EZEKIEL UNMASKED
A REVELATION
OF
YESHUA'S LOVE
JUSTICE
AND
REDEMPTION

Yeshua's Justice - Volume II
Chapter 25-39

P. D. DALLING

3G Publishing, Inc.
Loganville, GA 30052
www.3gpublishinginc.com
Phone: 1-888-442-9637

ISBN: 978-1-941247-18-1

Contents

.

About the Author

P.D. Dalling was born on the small island of Jamaica West Indies of both African and Jewish lineage. She was commissioned by the LORD to be a voice to the nations of the world through these inspired writings in these final hours of human history. A student of the Word, P.D Dalling was given several visions and dreams starting from the young age of five. The most intriguing of these visions was one given in consecutive order over a period of seven years showing the construction of an enormous temple from the laying of its foundation until the final stages of it being painted in gold. The author later realized that the vision was to prepare her for this assignment as she neared the completion of a six week teaching on *"The Justice of God."*

Prior to completing this series of teachings, the author once more sought Yeshua as she usually does for the next assignment. A few days later on a hot Saturday afternoon, a call came from a devoted Saint of God and watchman living in the State of Florida, who was unaware of the author's prayer request; this devoted follower of Yeshua Jesus shared a message received from the Lord at 2 A.M. that morning. "Tell My child to teach on the book of Ezekiel, it will be tough." The author accepted the challenge but was met with many obstacles and a wrestling In spirit as to the format for something of this magnitude. Then came the answer in a dream to the author; the Lord wanted this work to be put into writing.

P.D. Dalling had to rely on the leading and inner witness of Holy Spirit to begin and complete this project, as He explicitly spoke: "I will teach you." Indeed this was a very difficult task that took on a whole new meaning of what is meant: to have fellowship with Holy Spirit.

Because this work was commissioned by the LORD, P.D. Dalling refrains from offering any personal credentials or academic scholarship. All glory and honor goes to Abba Father, Yeshua Jesus His Son and my great teacher and friend Holy Spirit who will reward their bondservant in heaven.

Preface

The book of Ezekiel will take you on a prophetic journey from the day the LORD GOD called Ezekiel to be His voice to the nation of Israel in exile, unto these present times. Said to be the most intriguing and mysterious book of the Old Testament, there are two clear themes to its interpretation; the literal and the spiritual-prophetic. Psalm 12:6 states: The words of the LORD are pure words: as silver tried in a furnace of earth, purified seven times. This is a fair description of the depth of the interpretation of the book of Ezekiel, because it is given by inspiration and revelation of Holy Spirit. This work offers no preponderance for replacement theology. The book speaks of GOD'S dealings with Israel His people to the unification of the body of Yeshua with their Jewish brothers as One New Man (Ephesians 3). This work flows with GOD'S grace, mercy, and love for a people who rebelled against Him, worshiped other gods, and suffered at the hands of their oppressors. When they repented, like a loving Father, He forgives and reconcile with His beloved.

In the book of Ezekiel the LORD GOD sometimes spoke by the mouth of His prophet using metaphors, allegories, euphemisms, typologies, prophetic role play, analogies, and coded mysteries, which has frustrated readers of this book for centuries. At this time and by GOD'S own providence, He has broken the seal that clouds the mind to reveal divine truths in these last days. This work is presented in three volumes. Volume one covers chapters 1-24 and addresses Israel's past. Volume two covers chapters 25-39 and address Israel's present state and volume three covers chapters 40-48 unveiling Israel's glorious future and the adoption of the Gentiles into the generation of Yeshua Jesus. Yeshua's love, for His beloved people is revealed in volume one; His justice in laid out in volume two and His redemption in volume three. This compilation unmasks the spiritual prophetic content of the book of Ezekiel; it demonstrates the love of Abba Father for all people whom He created in His image and likeness and gives a final call for all to come out of this sin infested world and find rest in Him.

The LORD addresses both good and evil, shepherds and hirelings, the righteous and the unrighteous; leaders of Israel as well as leaders of other nations. Yeshua's suffering and His coming reign as the Prince of peace among His brethren is reveled in the book of Ezekiel. It will be this Prince; the Son of GOD, who will reunite man with Abba Father not as a god, but as ONE NEW MAN in Yeshua HaMashiach, Jesus the Messiah. Ephesians 2:11-15 and 3:1-6 are principal building block for this review on the forty-eight chapters of Ezekiel: *Wherefore remember, that ye being in time past Gentiles in the flesh, who are called Uncircumcision by that which is called the Circumcision in the flesh made by hands; that at that time ye were without Christ, being aliens from the commonwealth of Israel, and strangers from the covenants of promise, having no hope, and without God in the world: but now in Christ Jesus ye who sometimes were far off are made nigh by the blood of Christ. For He is our peace, who hath made both one, and broken down the middle wall of partition between us; having abolished in His flesh the enmity, even the law of commandments contained in ordinances; for to make in Himself of twain ONE NEW MAN, so making peace. . . . For this cause I Paul, the prisoner of Jesus Christ for you Gentiles, if ye have heard of the dispensation of the grace of God which is given me to you-ward: how that by revelation He made known unto me the mystery; (as I wrote afore in few words, whereby, when ye read, ye may understand my knowledge in the mystery of Christ) which in other ages was not made known unto the sons of men, as it is now revealed unto His holy apostles and prophets by the Spirit; That the Gentiles should be fellow heirs, and of the same body, and partakers of His promise in Christ by the gospel.*

As the construction of the temple of man takes shape in volume three of these writings, we will see the manifold grace of Abba Father unfolding. The tabernacle of Moses is a picture of the law or teachings, but the temple of Yeshua Jesus is all about the grace of His Father, which He extends to all. Romans 6:1-14 states: *What shall we say then? Shall we continue in sin, that grace may abound? God forbid. How shall we, that are dead to sin, live any longer therein? Know ye not, that so many of us as were baptized into Jesus Christ were baptized into His death? Therefore we are buried with Him by baptism into death: that like as Christ was raised up from the dead by the glory of the Father, even so we also should walk in newness of life. For if we have been planted together in the likeness of His death, we shall also be in the likeness of His resurrection: knowing this, that our old man is crucified with him, that the body of sin might be destroyed, that henceforth we should not serve sin. Now if we be dead with Christ, we believe that we shall also live with Him: knowing that Christ being raised from the dead dieth no more; death hath no more dominion over Him. For in that He died, He died unto sin once: but in that He liveth, He liveth unto God. Likewise reckon ye also yourselves to be dead indeed unto sin, but alive unto God through Jesus Christ our Lord. Let not sin therefore reign in your mortal body, that ye should obey it in the lusts thereof. Neither yield ye your members as instruments of unrighteousness unto sin: but yield yourself unto God, as those that are alive from the dead, and your members as instruments of righteousness unto God. For sin shall not have dominion over you: for ye are not under the law, but under grace.* The body of Yeshua Jesus, like Israel, is in spiritual exile, but the day will come as you will see step by step unfolding in the book of Ezekiel, when man will once again enjoy fellowship with God face to face.

The unmasking of the book of Ezekiel will bring about a radical change in the way Believers in Yeshua Jesus view Scriptures. It will rattle the conscience of the skeptic and shake the very foundation of Christian dogma. There are lengths, widths, heights and depths in the Word of God that are yet to be revealed. The LORD is waiting to take those who are willing to travel with Him from the surface of His Word and descend to its greatest depths but the choice is ours. Beneath the surface of the Word of God are wonders to behold, this however will be a lifelong task of total abandonment that comes at a great price. The deeper Yeshua takes us in the Word, will make the crushing greater and the judgment stricter, but in the end the natural man will be regenerated and the attributes of the Living God will radiate from his being thereby changing the lives of others. Ecclesiastes 1:9-10 applying the NKJV states: *That which has been is what will be, that which is done is what will be done, and there is nothing new under the sun. Is there anything of which it may be said, "See, this is new"? It has already been in ancient times before us.* As plans are being made for the third temple to be constructed in Jerusalem, God has already begun a parallel work in mankind by preparing us to be His spiritual abode to enter the kingdom of God and the New Jerusalem that comes down from heaven. This temple is therefore referred to as the fourth temple in these writings because it is not natural but spiritual.

Both Jews and Gentile Believers will understand their divine purpose as God reveals something about Himself and His relationship with mankind as He breaks the seal and reveals astounding truths from the Book of Ezekiel. Ezekiel unmasked is therefore God's message to Jews and Gentiles. He addresses our weaknesses and raises the bar to show our strengths. He places the ball labeled "choice" in our court as He motivates us to choose eternal life over death and lasting fellowship instead of damnation. If we accept His calling; He lifts us out of the mire of sin, declares us holy by His grace, and calls us kings and priests. He speaks of Israel as His firstborn and all those who believe in Yeshua Jesus, as been born-again! One day the body of Yeshua will share in the glorious inheritance of Israel as sons and daughters of the King of all kings and Lord of all lords.

God is building a temple

Not made by human hands

The blueprint designed in heaven

A revelation of ONE NEW MAN

Jews and Gentiles called by God to live in unity

Under the eternal banner of love for all the world to see

Both were bought and paid for at a very dear price

Yeshua's poured out blood became their perfect sacrifice.

P.D.Dalling, "A Temple Not Built By Human Hands."

Volume II

Israel's Present: Yeshua's Justice

Chapter 25

Verses 1-7

"*The word of the LORD came again unto me, saying, Son of man, set thy face against the Ammonites, and prophesy against them; and say unto the Ammonites, Hear the word of the Lord GOD; Thus saith the Lord GOD; Because thou saidst, Aha, against My sanctuary, when it was profaned; and against the land of Israel, when it was desolate; and against the house of Judah, when they went into captivity; Behold, therefore I will deliver thee to the men of the east for a possession, and they shall set their places in thee, and make their dwellings in thee: they shall eat thy fruit, and they shall drink thy milk. And I will make Rabbah a stable for camels, and the Ammonites a couching place for flocks: and ye shall know that I am the LORD. For thus saith the Lord GOD; Because thou hast clapped thine hands, and stamped with the feet, and rejoiced in heart with all thy despite against the land of Israel; Behold, therefore I will stretch out Mine hand upon thee, and will deliver thee for a spoil to the heathen; and I will cut thee off from the people, and I will cause thee to perish out of the countries: I will destroy thee; and thou shalt know that I am the LORD.*"

To rejoice over the calamity of another is not wise. King Solomon penned these words by divine inspiration: "*Don't wait in ambush at the home of the godly, and don't raid the house where the godly live. The godly may trip seven times, but they will get up again. But one disaster is enough to overthrow the wicked. Don't rejoice when your enemies fall; don't be happy when they stumble. For the LORD will be displeased with you and will turn His anger away from them*" (Proverbs 24:15-18, NLT). How appropriate, the LORD would not have spoken against the Ammonites if they were grieved over the destruction of Jerusalem and enslavement of Judah. The Ammonites rejoiced over Judah's calamity, so the LORD sent a word of rebuke and judgment upon them and the days of their own downfall was about to be revealed. Amos 1:13-15 states: "*Thus saith the LORD; For three transgressions of the children of Ammon and for four, I will not turn away the punishment thereof; because they have ripped up the women with child of Gilead, that they might enlarge their border: but I will kindle a fire in the wall of Rabbah, and it shall devour the palaces thereof, with shouting in the day of battle, with a tempest in the day of the whirlwind: and their king shall go into captivity, he and his princes together, saith the LORD.*"

There are two cities in the Old Covenant name Rabbah (Rabbath). First there was one located in the hills of Judah (Joshua 15:60) and another in Ammon (Deuteronomy 3:11; 2 Samuels 12:26); the latter was judged by the LORD and condemned. This judgment was extremely severe because the race of the Ammonites would eventually become extinct (Jeremiah 49:1-2).

Verses 8-11

"*Thus saith the Lord GOD; Because that Moab and Seir do say, Behold, the house of Judah is like unto all the heathen; Therefore, behold, I will open the side of Moab from the cities, from his cities which are on his frontiers, the glory of the country, Beth-jeshimoth, Baal-meon, and Kiriathaim, unto the men of the east with the Ammonites, and will give them in possession, that the Ammonites may not be remembered among the nations. And I will execute judgment upon Moab; and they shall know that I am the LORD.*"

The Moabites were next to be judged by the LORD. Seir however, is actually a mountainous region where the Edomites settled and they, too, would be subject to a penalty; but in these verses the LORD lays out the punishment for Moab. Like the Ammonites, the Moabites chastisement was similar because through war and oppression they also would be totally destroyed by the men of the east who were the Babylonians. The reason for this conjecture is based on three facts. First, the heathen nations found it quite amusing that the city of Jerusalem was seized by the Babylonians and its citizens enslaved. It can therefore be assumed that those who hated Israel occupied territories in close proximity to Jerusalem and were known to have expressed pleasure over the news of Israel's defeat. Secondly, the king of Babylon used divination to decide which of the two cities to attack first; Judah or Rabbah (Rabbath, KJV), a city of the Ammonites. Let's go back to Ezekiel 21:19-23 applying the NIV: *"Son of man, mark out two roads for the sword of the king of Babylon to take, both starting from the same country. Make a signpost where the road branches off to the city. Mark out one road for the sword to come against Rabbah of the Ammonites and another against Judah and fortified Jerusalem. For the king of Babylon will stop at the fork in the road, at the junction of the two roads, to seek an omen: he will cast lots with arrows, he will consult his idols, he will examine the liver. Into his right hand will come the lot for Jerusalem, where he is to set up battering rams, to give the command to slaughter, to sound the battle cry, to set battering rams against the gates, to build a ramp and to erect siege works. It will seem like a false omen to those who have pledge allegiance to him, but he will remind them of their guilt and take them captive."* It is clearly seen here that the king of Babylon had a choice to attack Judah or the Ammonites, but Judah was chosen not by the king's divination as he thought, but by the divine judgment of the LORD upon His people.

The third hypothesis is found in the interpretation of Nebuchadnezzar's dream by Daniel, an exile from Jerusalem who served in the king's palace: *"You, O king were watching; and behold, a great image! This great image, whose splendor was excellent, stood before you; and its form was awesome. This image's head was of fine gold . . . This is the dream. Now we will tell the interpretation of it before the king. You, O king, are a king of kings. For the God of heaven has given you a kingdom, power, strength, and glory; and wherefore the children of men dwell, or the beasts of the field and the birds of the heaven, He has given them into your hand, and has made you ruler over them all you are the head of Gold"* (Daniel 2:31, 32a, 36-38 NKJV).

Using the timelines of Daniel's interpretation of Nebuchadnezzar's dream, the men of the east most likely were the Babylonians, because the head of gold that was given dominion over the earth during that period of history was the Babylonian Empire. It can therefore be concluded that most likely the men from the east were Nebuchadnezzar's army. When the Babylonian army had completely subdued Judah, the Ammonites were their next target followed by the Moabites. The Edomites living in the mountainous region called Seir and also the Philistines would be punished later by another dynasty.

Verses 12-17

"Thus saith the Lord GOD; Because that Edom hath dealt against the house of Judah by taking vengeance, and hath greatly offended, and revenged himself upon them; therefore thus saith the Lord GOD; I will also stretch out Mine hand upon Edom, and will cut of man and beast from it; and I will make it desolate from Teman; and they of Dedan shall fall by the sword. And I will lay My vengeance upon Edom by the hand of My people Israel: and they shall do in Edom according to Mine anger and according to My fury; and they shall know My vengeance, saith the Lord GOD. Thus saith the Lord GOD; Because the Philistines have dealt by revenge, and have taken vengeance with a despiteful heart, to destroy it for the old hatred; therefore thus saith the Lord GOD; Behold, I will stretch out Mine hand upon the Philistines, and I will cut off the Cherethims, and destroy the remnant of the sea coast. And I will execute great vengeance upon them with furious rebukes; and they shall know that I am the LORD, when I shall lay My vengeance upon them."

The Lord was displeased with the actions of the Edomites who were descendants of Esau, Jacob's brother. These cousins of Israel refused to offer assistance to their kindred and instead, they sided with Israel's enemies. The prophet Amos wrote: *"Thus saith the LORD; for three transgressions of Edom, and for four, I will not turn away the punishment thereof; because he did pursue his brother with a sword, and did cast off all pity, and his anger did tear perpetually, and he kept his wrath forever: but I will send a fire upon Teman, which shall devour the palaces of Bozrah"* (1:11-12).

Edom's geographical location formed a natural fortress, but this would not impede the punishment of the LORD. His retribution would be swift and thorough, and it would come from Israel, the people they least feared. Isaiah 11:10-14 states: *"Then it will happen on that day that the Lord will again recover the second time with His hand the remnant of His people, who will remain from Assyria, Egypt, Pathros, Cush, Elam, Shinar, Hamath, and from the islands of the sea. And He will lift up a standard for the nations and assemble the banished ones of Israel, and will gather the dispersed of Judah from the four corners of the earth. Then the jealousy of Ephraim will depart, and those who harass Judah will be cut off; Ephraim will not be jealous of Judah and Judah will not harass Ephraim. They will swoop down on the slopes of the Philistines on the west; together they will plunder the sons of the east; they will possess Edom and Moab and the sons of Ammon will be subject to them"* (NASB). The nations looked upon Israel as being small and insignificant, but they forgot one important thing: the God of Israel is also the LORD God of the universe.

Because of hatred and a grudge that passed down through the ages, the Cherethims (Cherethites) who were close allies of the Philistines joined forces with them to fight against Israel without a cause. The delay of the LORD's judgment on Edom, the Philistine and their allies the Cherethites, would one day be recompensed and this would be a sign to all that the downfall of the enemies of Israel was not by tactical maneuvers, but by the favor of Abba Father because they were outnumbered in battle.

Chapter 26

Verses 1-18

"And it came to pass in the eleventh year, in the first day of the month, that the word of the LORD came unto me, saying, Son of man, because that Tyrus hath said against Jerusalem, Aha, she is broken that was the gates of the people: she is turned unto me: I shall be replenished, now she is laid waste: therefore thus saith the Lord GOD; Behold, I am against thee, O Tyrus, and will cause many nations to come up against thee, as the sea causeth his waves to come up. And they shall destroy the walls of Tyrus, and break down her towers: I will also scrape her dust from her, and make her like a top of a rock. It shall be a place for the spreading of nets in the midst of the sea: for I have spoken it, saith the Lord GOD: and it shall become a spoil to the nations. And her daughters which are in the field shall be slain by the sword; and they shall know that I am the LORD. For thus saith the Lord GOD; Behold, I will bring upon Tyrus Nebuchadnezzar king of Babylon, a king of kings, from the north, with horses, and with chariots, and with horsemen, and companies, and much people. He shall slay with the sword thy daughters in the field: and he shall make a fort against thee, and cast a mount against thee, and lift up the buckler against thee. And he shall set engines of war against thy walls, and with his axes he shall break down thy towers. By reason of the abundance of his horses their dust shall cover thee: thy walls shall shake at the noise of the horsemen, and of the wheels, and of the chariots, when he shall enter into thy gates, as men enter into a city wherein is made a breach. With the hoofs of his horses shall he tread down all thy streets: he shall slay thy people by the sword, and thy strong garrisons shall go down to the ground. And they shall make a spoil of thy riches, and make a prey of thy merchandise: and they shall break down thy walls, and destroy thy pleasant houses: and they shall lay thy stones and thy timber and thy dust in the midst of the water. And I will cause the noise of thy songs to cease; and the sound of thy harps shall be no more heard. And I will make thee like the top of a rock: thou shalt be a place to spread nets upon; thou shalt be built no more: for I the LORD have spoken it, saith the Lord GOD. Thus saith the Lord GOD to Tyrus; shall not the isles shake at the sound of thy fall, when the wounded cry, when the slaughter is made in the midst of thee? Then all the princes of the sea shall come down from their thrones, and lay away their robes, and put off their broidered garments: they shall clothe themselves with trembling; they shall sit upon the ground, and shall tremble at every moment, and be astonished at thee. And they shall take up a lamentation for thee, and say to thee, How art thou destroyed, that wast inhabited of seafaring men, the renowned city, which wast strong in the sea, she and her inhabitants, which caused their terror to be on all that haunt it! Now shall the isles tremble in the day of thy fall; yea, the isles that are in the sea shall be troubled at thy departure."

Ezekiel the prophet gives an oracle declaring the destruction of Tyrus, but before exploring these verses let's examine some important facts about this mainland to lay a foundation. Tyrus also called Zera, Tyros, and Tyre means "rock," a fitting name which described the features of its coastland. This affluent city with its rocky terrain and natural topography made it quite difficult to be invaded. To the east of Tyrus was a rocky mountain cliff and to its west was the Mediterranean Sea. Lying to its north was the land of Israel and less than a day's journey, which is about twenty-five miles, was Sidon (Zidon). Because of the very close proximity of Tyre and Sidon, we see both mentioned together frequently in Scripture.

Some theologians indicate that Tyrus was first mentioned in Joshua 19:29 but that is not so. As a matter of fact, Tyrus was first alluded to in the book of Genesis as Jacob (Israel), blessed his sons. Genesis 49:13 states: "Zebulun will live by the seashore and become a haven for ships; his border will extend toward Sidon" (NIV). Prior to his death, Moses also spoke a blessing for Zebulun: "And of Zebulun he said, "Rejoice, Zebulun, in thy going out, and, Issachar in thy tents! They shall call the peoples to the mountain; there they shall offer sacrifices of righteousness; for they shall partake of the abundance of the seas and of treasures hidden in the sand" (Deuteronomy 33:18-19 NKJV). Here we see both Zebulun and Issachar mentioned together: "Zebulun *is thy going out, and, Issachar in thy tents."* "*Going out,*" is another word for sea-fearing. Both Jacob and Moses blessed Zebulun and gave him Tyrus but something happened because Asher inherited it instead. What occurred that caused Zebulun to forfeit his blessing? Let's go to Joshua 18:1-3: "*Now the whole congregation of the children of Israel assembled together at Shiloh, and set up the tabernacle of meeting there. And the land was subdued before them. But there remained among the children of Israel seven tribes which had not yet received their inheritance. Then Joshua said unto the children of Israel. "How long will you neglect to go and possess the land which the LORD GOD of your fathers has given you?"* (See also Joshua 19:10-51). By these words of Joshua it showed that the land given to the sons of Jacob were not all taken. The LORD now steps in and re-distributes the land Himself. Joshua 18:6-10; 19:10-16, 24-31 shows the land redistribution for Zebulun and Asher, with Asher and his descendants being allocated the fortified city of Tyrus, which was previously given to his brother Zebulun (Joshua 19:29). Leah was ecstatic at the birth of Zebulun because he was a gift to her from GOD as his name implies (Genesis 30:19-20). There is however a deeper meaning as it relates to this special child. Leah did all she could to be first in her husband's heart but that place was reserved for her younger sister Rachel. The LORD knew this and Zebulun was a dowry from Him to Leah, indicating that although she was not her husband's first love, she was in fact first place in the eyes of the LORD, so He justly gave this child to her as a dowry; the gift brought by the bride to her husband at the time of marriage, and Zebulun was that gift.

The LORD makes no mistake, He is intimately aware of everything both good and evil. Zebulun forfeited his gift and at the death of his father and later Moses, this gift was transferred to his brother Asher, the surrogate son of Leah by her handmaid Zilpah. The name Asher is interpreted "happy" (Genesis 30:12-13) and that which Zebulun failed to possess as a free gift, made someone else very happy. The wealthy Phoenician trading at port of Tyrus now belonged to Asher, but he, too, failed to completely rid the land of heathen settlers (Judges Chapter 1). The LORD knows the devastating effect of co-mingling with the ungodly, and for this reason, He would always warn His people to completely cleanse the land prior to its occupation. Throughout Scripture the ill-effect of not thoroughly removing every trace of the previous inhabitants from a region as ordered by the LORD, have caused

Israel to be repeatedly influenced by their idolatrous cultural practices.

Verses 19-21

"For thus saith the Lord GOD; When I shall make thee a desolate city, like the cities that are not inhabited; when I shall bring up the deep upon thee, and great waters shall cover thee; when I shall bring thee down with them that descend into the pit, with the people of old time, and shall set thee in the lower parts of the earth, in places desolate of old, with them that go down to the pit, that thou be not inhabited; and I shall set glory in the land of the living; I will make thee a terror, and thou shalt be no more: though thou be sought for, yet shalt thou never be found again, saith the Lord GOD."

The Babylonian incursion on Tyrus was devastating, yet this great and affluent city-state whose geographical location was its strength and security, would be brought low once again and this time they would be dealt a final, crushing defeat. The LORD said He would bring up the deep and great waters upon Tyre, metaphorically speaking of allowing another nation to complete their final and crushing blow to their already war-wearied state. Alexander III popularly known as Alexander the Great, 356-323 B.C., founder of Alexandria and King of Macedon conquered Tyrus. Flavius Josephus, a Romano-Jewish historian confirmed that it was Alexander the Great who accomplished this feat (*"Josephus" The Complete Works* p. 11.8.4). As Tyrus became rejected, debased and discarded, so also was the memories of this once glorious city state.

Chapter 27

Verses 1-36

"The word of the LORD came again unto me, saying, Now, thou son of man, take up a lamentation for Tyrus; and say unto Tyrus, O thou that art situate at the entry of the sea, which art a merchant of the people for many isles, thus saith the Lord GOD; O Tyrus, thou hast said, I am of perfect beauty. Thy borders are in the midst of the seas, thy builders have perfected thy beauty. They have made all thy ship boards of fir trees of Senir: they have taken cedars from Lebanon to make masts for thee. Of the oaks of Bashan have they made thine oars; the company of the Ashurites have made thy benches of ivory, brought out of the isles of Chittim. Fine linen with broidered work from Egypt was that which thou spreadest forth to be thy sail; blue and purple from the isles of Elishah was that which covered thee. The inhabitants of Zidon and Arvad were thy mariners: thy wise men, O Tyrus, that were in thee, were thy pilots. The ancients of Gebal and the wise men thereof were in thee thy calkers: all the ships of the sea with their mariners were in thee to occupy thy merchandise. They of Persia and of Lud and of Put were in thine army, thy men of war: they hanged their shield and helmet in thee; they set forth thy comeliness. The men of Arvad with thine army were upon thy walls round about, and the Gammadims were in thy towers: they hanged their shields upon thy walls round about; they have made thy beauty perfect. Tarshish was thy merchant by reason of the multitude of all kind of riches; with silver, iron, tin, and lead, they traded in thy fairs. Javan, Tubal, and Meshech, they were thy merchants: they traded the persons of men and vessels of brass in thy markets. They of the house of Togarmah traded in thy fairs with horses and horsemen and mules. The men of Dedan were thy merchants; many isles were the merchandise of thine hand: they brought thee for a present horns of ivory and ebony.

Syria was thy merchant by reason of the multitude of thy wares of thy making: they occupied in thy fairs with emeralds, purple, and broidered work, and fine linen, and coral, and agate. Judah and the land of Israel, they were thy merchants: they traded in thy market wheat on Minnith, and pannag, and honey, and oil, and balm. Damascus was thy merchant in the multitude of thy wares of thy making, for the multitude of all riches; in the wine of Helbon and white wool. Dan also and Javan going to and fro occupied thy fairs: bright iron, cassia, and calamus, were in thy market. Dadan was thy merchant in precious clothes for chariots. Arabia, and all the princes of Kedar, they occupied with thee in lambs, and rams, and goats: in thee were they thy merchants. The merchants of Sheba and Raamah, they were thy merchants: they occupied in thy fares with chief of all spices, and with all precious stones, and gold. Haran, and Canneh, and Eden, the merchants of Sheba, Asshur, and Chilmad, were thy merchants. These were thy merchants in all sort of things, in blue clothes and broidered work, and in chests of rich apparel, bound with cords, and made of cedar, among thy merchandise. The ships of Tarshish did sing of thee in thy market: and thou wast replenished, and made very glorious in the midst of the seas. Thy rowers have brought thee into great waters: the east wind hath broken thee in the midst of the seas. Thy riches, and thy fairs, thy merchandise, thy mariners, and thy pilots, thy calkers, and the occupiers of thy merchandise, and all thy men of war, that are in thee, and in all thy company which is in the midst of thee, shall fall into the midst of the seas in the day of thy ruin. The suburbs shall shake at the sound of the cry of thy pilots. And all that handle the oar, the mariners, and all the pilots of the sea, shall come down from their ships, they shall stand upon the land; and shall cause their voice to be heard against thee, and shall cry bitterly, and shall cast up dust upon their heads, they shall wallow themselves in the ashes: and they shall make themselves utterly bald for thee, and gird them with sackcloth, and they shall weep for thee in bitterness of heart and bitter wailing. And in their wailing they shall take up a lamentation for thee, and lament over thee, saying, What city is like Tyrus, like the destroyed in the midst of the sea? When thy wares went forth out of the seas, thou filledst many people; thou didst enrich the kings of the earth with the multitude of thy riches and thy merchandise. In the time when thou shalt be broken by the seas in the depths of the waters thy merchandise and all thy company in the midst of thee shall fall. All the inhabitants *of the isles shall be astonished at thee, and their kings shall be sore afraid, they shall be troubled in their countenance. The merchants among the people shall hiss at thee, thou shall be a terror, and never shalt be any more."*

What had become of Tyrus? This great affluent and influential port, famous in the known world for their marketing skills, commerce and slave trade, was about to crash, never to rise again. The leaders of the city were shrewd financial advisors who were trusted for their unique trading skills, but all this was coming to an end by those who envied them. Tyrus' downfall was a direct result of the chastisement of God. Their vast and diversified empire, patronized by kings, nobles and peasants would fall hard (1Kings 5:1-10). There were approximately thirty-five nations, which included some cities that wound be dumbfounded as they mourned the sudden toppling of this once powerful and very popular transshipment port. Its leaders, merchants and business partners became corrupt by their vast wealth which led to pride, and the subtle, yet methodical dismantling of everything in the nation that bore the name of God. There is so much that we can learn from the economic collapse of Tyrus:

- As we prosper; celebrate the LORD for His goodness because it is He who makes it possible.
- Stay away from conceit; trusting in one's own possessions is arrogant and the first step that leads to the total collapse of one's wealth at an unpredictable moment, therefore discovering one's mistake a little too late.
- Whatever we plant that we will also reap.
- Never accept the worship of men; it amounts to idolatry which the LORD God will judge.
- Never rejoice over the calamities of others; it brings displeasure to the LORD (Proverbs 24:17-18).

Tyrus' fall was great because the hearts of its leaders was filled with pride and envy, thereby opening the gateway to a supernatural evil force known as the King of Tyrus. This principality founded pleasure in Tyrus' pain and the reason was based on the fact that this once prosperous nation that traded in the past with king Solomon of Judah in the construction of the second temple in Jerusalem, rejoiced over Israel's fall and subsequent exile (1 Kings 5:1-10; Ezekiel 26:2-7). The LORD did not take this gloating lightly, so Tyrus was handed over to be punished by their tormentors who in essence, they truly belonged. Those who condemn Israel, the elect of God, will also in like manner be condemned by Abba Father the Great Judge who is intimately acquainted with the propensity of all mankind.

Chapter 28

Verses 1-2

"The word of the LORD came again unto me, saying, Son of man, say unto the prince of Tyrus, thus saith the Lord GOD; Because thine heart is lifted up, and thou hast said, I am a God, I sit in the seat of God, in the midst of the seas; yet thou art a man, and not God, thou hast set thine heart as the heart of God."

The LORD changes His focus to the prince of Tyrus who was a leader of great renown and nobility. He is referred to as "prince" because his behavior, as well as his rulings were directly influenced by a dark evil spiritual kingdom and powerful principality known as the King of Tyrus. The nations of the earth depended upon Tyrus and this great leader was the bread basket to their existence. This once glorious nation had leaders who in times past, served the God of Abraham when they were small and ignoble. In 1 Kings 5:7, Hiram a leader who once governed Tyre acknowledged the Sovereignty of GOD as the verse states: *"When Hiram heard the words of Solomon, he rejoiced greatly and said, "Blessed be the LORD today, who has given to David a wise son over this great people"* (NASB). Hiram blessed the LORD, and declared His goodness. Noticed he said *"Blessed be the LORD today."* This salutation ran much deeper than formality because Hiram was kin to David and Solomon, being the son of a widow from the tribe of Naphtali, the sixth son of Jacob by Rachel's handmaiden Bilhah (1 Kings 7:13-14). As time went by and the city-state became a famous transshipment port, their succeeding leaders forgot the LORD and boasted in the abundance of their wares, the snare that led to their ultimate destruction.

When Tyrus sustained the last and fatal blow to its economy, Hiram was already dead. Important information found in the Word of God gives us timelines proving that Tyrus was already in a state of apostasy when their destruction came. Solomon ruled over the house of Israel for forty years during Hiram's time (2 Chronicles 9:30) and when Tyre fell Jerusalem was already under siege (2 Chronicles 36:4-7). Using this information as a point of reference and adding the number of years each king ruled after Solomon, including Jehoiakim who reigned at the time of the siege; over four hundred and sixteen years had passed and unrepentant idolatry and sin progressed to the moral and spiritual decline of the people. The worship of the LORD slowly disappeared from Tyrus as lawlessness, oppression, war and poverty ensued. Proverbs 8:13 and 16:18 applying the NKJV states: "*The fear of the LORD is to hate evil; pride and arrogance and the evil way, and the perverse mouth I hate. . . . Pride goeth before destruction and a haughty spirit before a fall.*" These words became a witness against the prince of Tyrus because he forgot the LORD God who made them prosper.

This prince of Tyrus had it made, yet lost it all because he consulted with the dark arts, thinking in his heart that evil was more pleasurable than doing that which is pleasing and honorable. His great successes and the accolades of the surrounding nations got to his head and with his heart lifted up, he recklessly elevated himself to the status of God (Exodus 20:2-3). This once great and notable leader slowly drifted from the kingdom of light into the kingdom of darkness. Over the process of time, there was no trace of God left in him and his adoption into the kingdom of darkness was complete, thereby earning him the title, "prince," a natural agitator influenced by a supernatural evil fallen being.

Verses 3-10

"*Behold, thou art wiser than Daniel; there is no secret that they can hide from thee: with thy wisdom and with thine understanding thou hast gotten thee riches, and hast gotten gold and silver into thy treasures: by thy great wisdom and by thy traffick hast thou increased thy riches, and thine heart is lifted up because of thy riches: therefore thus saith the Lord GOD; because thou hast set thine heart as the heart of God; behold, therefore I will bring strangers upon thee, the terrible of the nations: and they shall draw their swords against the beauty of thy wisdom, and they shall defile thy brightness. They shall bring thee down to the pit, and thou shalt die the deaths of them that are slain in* the midst of the seas. Wilt thou yet say before him that slayeth thee, I am God? But thou shalt be a man, and no God, in the hand of him that slayeth thee. Thou shalt die the deaths of the uncircumcised by the hands of strangers: for I have spoken it, saith the Lord GOD."

The address to the prince of Tyrus, the leader of the nation continues. The LORD revealed to Ezekiel that the wisdom and understanding of the prince outshined that of Daniel because He, the LORD, had made him so. There is however a marked difference between the prince's wisdom and that of Daniel as the LORD also stated that the prince's wisdom was tainted by pride (28:2). In Daniel chapter two, Nebuchadnezzar had a puzzling dream which he could not remember, but earnestly wanted those possessing the art of interpretation of omens and dreams in his kingdom, not only to tell him what the dream was, but also to explain it. Daniel sought the LORD, and He revealed to him the dream as well as its interpretation. Before explaining the dream to Nebuchadnezzar, Daniel declared unto the king, the Sovereignty of the Lord thereby making it known that the dream and its interpretation was not acquired by any innate ability, but by the all-knowing GOD of heaven and earth: "...The secret which the king has demanded, the wise men, the astrologers, the magicians, and the soothsayers cannot declare to the king. But there is a God in heaven who reveals secrets, and He has made known to King Nebuchadnezzar what will be in the later days..." (2:27-28).

Daniel's excellent qualities never wavered, he gave credit to the God of heaven for his divine gift, unlike the prince of Tyre. Daniel was humble. He possessed the Spirit of God. Light and understanding was in him and he had an exceptionally good spirit of the highest and finest quality ever seen in Babylon marked by his ability to interpret and solve difficult dreams, puzzling visions and riddles. This was only a part of his impressive portfolio which he consistently used to glorify God. The leader of Tyrus on the other hand was said to have possessed a far greater gift than that of Daniel which made him prosper. Unlike Daniel however, this prince enjoyed the attention he received from others as well as his love and admiration for himself. Consumed with pride and a successful business empire bar none, the prince of Tyrus basked in the glory and worship of his fellowmen, an honor that was reserved for God alone. This fatal error had dire consequences, which transcends time, because another famous king hundreds of years later would also make the same deadly mistake.

As the Roman Empire flourish, the same could not be said about Tyre and Sidon that had now become poor, abased and receiving welfare from Rome. Let's see what happened to Herod as he failed to give honor and glory to the LORD. Acts 12:20-23 records this strange and frightening account: "*Now Herod had been very angry with the people of Tyre and Sidon; but they came to him with one accord, and having made Blastus the king's personal aide their friend, they asked for peace, because their country was supplied with food by the king's country. So on a set day Herod, arrayed in royal apparel, sat on his throne and gave an oration to them. And the people kept shouting, "The voice of a god and not a man!" Then immediately an angel of the Lord struck him because he did not give glory to God. And he was eaten by worms and died*"(NKJV).

This earthly king attempted to exalt himself as God; but instantly found himself in a bed of worms until his death. The prince of the nation of Tyre was also prideful and so sealed his own fate. In the supernatural realm, there was a powerful fallen angel known by many names and titles including Lucifer, who along with a very large number of angels attempted insurrection against the LORD God his Creator, desiring to be heralded as king. If such a powerful arch angel along with other angelic beings failed to overthrow the kingdom of GOD, how likely would it be for even the most powerful human created a little lower than the angels accomplish such a feat?

We know that the LORD was addressing a human and not a spiritual being, because it is so stated in Ezekiel 28:2-5. It was by the extraordinary intellectual and creative genius of this leader, one that surpassed that of Daniel that made Tyrus so famous but he had a weakness called pride, which wormed itself like cancer into his unusual abilities and made the nation vulnerable to those who craved their wealth and power for themselves. At an appointed time, Tyrus' final destruction came at the hands of Alexander the Great and his army (see Josephus 11.8.4).

Unlike Daniel, the prince of Tyrus enjoyed the attention and priceless gifts lavished upon him by others because of his wisdom, never remembering to acknowledge God for his unequaled abilities. This love and obsession for himself and his riches was a venomous concoction that was lethal in its sting, because it drove the prince into the jaws of the abyss being condemned with the uncircumcised. Circumcision is the surgical removing of the foreskin, but its purpose runs much deeper because it is a blood covenant between Abba Father and His people (Genesis 17; Deuteronomy 10:16; Jeremiah 4:4). It identifies Israel as belonging to Abba Father and a command that He alone they should honor and serve. The act of circumcision is therefore a unique contract between the LORD and the house of Israel.

To be called uncircumcised, meant that a person had no covenant with GOD; neither in the ceremonial rite of circumcision nor the state of one's heart. In Ezekiel 28:10, the LORD used "uncircumcised," thereby adding this prince to the list of unrighteous leaders. The prince of Tyrus and his famous city would one day be utterly defeated and the renown of this transshipment port would never rise to its former glory (for further reading see Isaiah chapter 23). Zechariah 9:2b-4 applying the NASB states: *"Tyre and Sidon, though they are very wise. For Tyre built for herself a fortress and piled up silver like dust, and gold like the mire of the streets. Behold the Lord will dispossess her and cast her wealth into the sea; and she will be consumed with fire."* Tyre the city state was influenced by an unseen evil presence and ruler named the king of Tyrus, which is none other than Satan himself.

Verses 11-19

"Moreover the word of the LORD came unto me, saying, Son of man, take up a lamentation upon the king of Tyrus, and say unto him, Thus saith the Lord GOD; thou sealest up the sum, full of wisdom, and perfect in beauty. Thou hast been in Eden the garden of God; every precious stone was thy covering, the sardius, topaz, and the diamond, the beryl, the onyx, and the jasper, the sapphire, the emerald, and the carbuncle, and gold: the workmanship of thy tabrets and of thy pipes was prepared in thee the day that thou wast created. Thou art the anointed cherub that covereth; and I have set thee so: thou wast upon the holy mountain of God; thou hast walked up and down in the midst of the stones of fire. Thou wast perfect in thy ways from the day that thou wast created, till iniquity was found in

thee. By the multitude of thy merchandise they have filled the midst of thee with violence, and thou hast sinned: therefore I will cast thee as profane out of the mountain of God: and I will destroy thee, O covering cherub, from the midst of the stones of fire. Thine heart was lifted up because of thy beauty, thou hast corrupted thy wisdom by reason of thy brightness: I will cast thee to the ground, I will lay thee before kings, that they may behold thee. Thou hast defiled thy sanctuaries by the multitude of thine iniquities, by the iniquity of thy traffick; therefore will I bring forth a fire from the midst of thee, it shall devour thee, and I will bring thee as ashes upon the earth in the sight of all them that behold thee. All they that know thee among the people shall be astonished at thee: thou shalt be a terror, and never shalt thou be any more."

The LORD judged the prince of Tyrus, now He turns His focus upon the King of Tyrus, a spiritual being that governs the realm of the second heaven. He is known by some of these names and titles: the dragon, the old serpent, the devil, Satan and Lucifer. In this rebuke, the LORD's closing argument examined the past, present and future of this spiritual being here called the King of Tyrus. The actions of the earthly leader or prince of Tyrus were directly influenced by this spiritual entity: like father like son, so to speak. In Ezekiel 28:14, the identity of the king is revealed to be the once anointed Cherub. He is described as being created, therefore he has no authority of his own. His authority is obtained from two sources: the LORD God his Creator whom he rebelled against, and mankind whom he continues to deceive by manipulation, infiltration, occupation and finally domination. Satan's warfare is against the soul of man and if this area of our tripartite being is not controlled by Holy Spirit, it becomes the playground of our adversary, which is this fallen one who wants humans to share in his final destruction.

There is no love in hell and those who have been deceived by the devil fail to realize that he is the author of lies (John 8:44). In reality, Satan truly hates mankind because of the uniqueness of our creation, and here is the proof. Genesis 1:26 and 3:14 states: *"Then God said, "Let Us make man in Our image, according to Our likeness; and let them rule over the fish of the sea and over the birds of the sky and over the cattle and over all the earth, and over every creeping thing that creeps on the earth"* . . . The LORD GOD said to the serpent, "Because you have done this,*

36

cursed are you more than all cattle, and more than every beast of the field; _on your belly you will go_, and dust you will eat all the days of your life."_ That which creeps in Genesis 1:26 also refers to the curse of this fallen Cherub, which is the serpent being on his belly in Genesis 3:14. Mankind was given authority over all the earth, and this also includes the fallen Cherub but nevertheless, he has been able to manipulate humans through ignorance and fear and continues to do so. His mind games must be resisted and the only way that this can be accomplished is by having fellowship with God (James 4:7-17). That which this fallen one offers is not his to give in the first place, neither is it a lasting reality. Mankind continues to be conned by Satan, whose true goal is to separate us from the love of God and our heavenly home. Everlasting torment was never the Lord's desire for people, but for the devil and his angels (Mathew 25:41).

A lamentation was made for the devil, the king of Tyrus because he would never again grace the presence of Almighty GOD as a worshiper, but as an accuser of the Saints. His precious stones and brightness was now transformed to charcoal because he rebelled. Although the Cherubim (plural) are associated with worship, they are also created to be protectors. The command given to Moses by the LORD recorded in Exodus 25:18-22 applying the NKJV states: _"And you shall make two cherubim of gold; of hammered work you shall make them at the two ends of the mercy seat. Make one cherub at one end, and the other cherub at the other end; you shall make the cherubim at the two ends of it of one piece with the mercy seat. And the cherubim shall stretch out their wings above, covering the mercy seat with their wings, and they shall face one another, the faces of the cherubim shall be toward the mercy seat. You shall put the mercy seat on top of the ark, and in the ark you shall put the Testimony that I will give you. And there I will meet with you, and I will speak with you from above the mercy seat, from between the two cherubim which are on the ark of the Testimony, about everything which I will give you in commandment to the children of Israel"_ (see also 37:6-9). The teachings of the LORD were placed in the ark, which was then covered by the mercy seat. On top of the mercy seat were replicas of the Cherubim; they were the protectors or guards, who watched over the Word of God, ready to be dispatched to fulfill its utterance on a moment's notice on the behalf of mankind.

The ark was a container which symbolically speaks of the heart, Psalm 119:11 states: "*Thy word have I hid in mine heart, that I might not sin against Thee.*" Instead of guarding the Word of God, this Cherub called the king of Tyrus, twisted, polluted, corrupted and attempted to destroy mankind by his everlasting desire to rid the earth of the Word. The next function of the Cherub is the worship of Abba Father continually without ceasing. When we worship the Lord GOD, our adversary flees because worship is initiated at the throne of God where the living Word lives and this fallen one is prohibited to enter.

The Word reaches farther and deeper than being spoken or written. The Word is a person whose name is Yeshua Jesus, our Messiah. It is said of Him, "*In the beginning was the Word, and the Word was with God, and the Word was God. He was in the beginning with God. All things were made through Him, and without Him nothing was made that were made. In Him was life, and the life was the light of men. . . . The life was manifested, and we have seen, and bear witness, and declare to you that eternal life which was with the Father and was manifested to us that which we have seen and heard we declare to you, that you also may have fellowship with us; and truly our fellowship is with the Father and with His Son Jesus Christ*" (John 1:1-4; 1 John 1:2-3 NKJV). This created being was once morally upright, but became absorbed with his unique and breathtaking creation. Desiring the attention and worship of everyone, he corrupted his wisdom.

The fallen Cherub once lived in the presence of the Almighty God offering worship, glory, and adoration but perverseness and dishonesty was gradually consuming his purity. He wanted to be worshiped as God, therefore he oppressed, misused his authority, and cast doubt in the hearts of men in an attempt to gain worship that is due only to the Creator. This fallen Cherub was also successful in perverting a large host of other angelic beings and they too, became morally corrupt themselves. The ultimate goal of this disgraced Cherub's scheming was to gain unlawful access to the throne of God, to sit above God and to be worshipped as God.

This angelic being was lavishly created with precious stones and the ability to emanate melodious praise unto the LORD God that could be heard throughout the kingdom of heaven. This must have had a tremendous impact on everyone, because he was anointed to do so. As all of heaven worship the LORD, this Cherub craved to be honored himself, because it was from his own body that these melodious sounds filled the atmosphere of GOD's kingdom. He must have said in his heart, "Why not worship me, I am the one from whom this melody is being poured out all over heaven," so he devised a plan to overthrow the kingdom of God. Was he aware that the One who created him knew everything about him? Angels as well as humans, were given the power of choice and therefore the potential to decide which path to take whether good or evil, (for further reading see Isaiah 14:13-15). The LORD is gracious, if He created angels and humans without the capacity to choose, then His Sovereignty would be questionable. We prove our love, devotion and desire to serve Him and to live in His presence by our own choosing and because of this, we see His everlasting justice as well as His immeasurable grace on display towards mankind because we were created with a soul that carries a redemptive component.

This fallen Cherub was covered with nine precious stones and the metal gold from which his musical sounds resonated. Gold is a symbol of the divine nature of GOD, whose holiness was woven into this angelic being when he was created. The source of his pride was his unique covering of precious stones and dazzling gold, but this very attribute that was once the source of his uniqueness was about to cost him everything. He was stripped of his magnificent stature and cast from the presence of Abba Father. His burning was described as that of lightening, and as he fell his glowing beauty was consumed by the fire of GOD's judgment. This Cherub had a measure of the divine wisdom of God, but through pride and obsession with himself, he became corrupt. Throughout the history of mankind, Satan has still been able to manipulate and taint our natural creativity especially in the area of the arts. Those who seek fame at any cost, fall victim to this disgraced Cherub's schemes as they, too, are prideful and in so doing accept that which Yeshua Jesus rejected when He was tempted of the devil (Matthew 4:3-11).

All dark revelation and commitment to this fallen being may seem pleasurable at first but this is the bait that lures mankind. The ultimate aim of this enemy of mankind, created by the Lord in His image and likeness, is to steal, kill and destroy our soul in hell (John 10:10). Satan promises the prideful in heart great honor in exchange for their soul, which they willingly agree to, not knowing that their fame will come at a great price. Unknown to them will be the ever presence of tormenting demons, because they are a part of the deal. These evil spirits will be their chaperone and overshadowing until the day they die if they do not renounce Satan's lordship and at their death he will send his entourage to escort them to meet their true master in hell. Whomever we pledge allegiance to, will be the one we will serve, not only in this world, but also the world to come. The twisting and polluting of the gifts given to mankind by God, started with the fall of this corrupt Cherub.

The king of Tyrus, whom Scripture identifies as the fallen Cherub, was a guardian in Eden. He was a protector, but out of envy and hatred, instead of protecting the human family, he intentionally deceived them by enticing Adam and Eve to disobey the LORD, thereby defiling his purpose and position as a Cherub that protects. The sin of Adam and Eve led to the fall of mankind because this fallen angel's ultimate goal was to destroy the first family by having them eat from the tree of life as well (Genesis 3:22), which would result in a perpetual fallen state. After the fall of this disgraced Cherub; the LORD God placed other Cherubim in Eden to keep away intruders from the tree of life. Man had already eaten from the tree of knowledge of good and evil and nothing they proposed in their heart would be impossible (Genesis 2:9; 3:1-7).

It is important to note that the Lord created this Cherub using nine precious stones and not twelve, because twelve stones were set aside for Yeshua Jesus the true High Priest (Hebrews 5:1-10). The high priest in the Old Covenant was a typology of Yeshua; his official vestment was designed with twelve stones in the breastplate (Exodus 28:1-2, 13-21). Was this Cherub jealous that the vestments of the high priest, and the true High Priest, Yeshua Jesus had twelve stones and his had only nine? Was he also jealous that Yeshua has the authority to judge and he did not (Revelation 19:11-16)? Was he jealous of man, because the man in Yeshua Jesus is a royal priesthood unto God? Was he jealous that his three missing stones revealed Yeshua's relationship with all mankind, which also declares the establishment of His future reign on the earth with them, a position he would never attain? Twelve is the number of perfection. The foundations of the New Jerusalem are built upon twelve stones found in Yeshua Jesus.

The number nine in Scripture means it is settled, it is finished; it is complete! This fallen Cherub, the dragon, the old serpent, was created with nine stones, the mark of his completion.

Yeshua is our High priest in Heaven while the man in Yeshua is His chosen people, His royal priesthood, His holy nation, and His own special people on earth (see 1 Peter 2:9). Here, we can clearly see why mankind is so hated and our chief enemy is working overtime to keep us deceived. Yeshua Jesus is the true Judge and He will judge all things in righteousness. The Apostle Paul in speaking to the men of Athens, whom some were worshipers of idols made of gold, silver, and stone said of Yeshua: *"For in Him we live and move and have our being, as also some of your poets have said, 'For we are also His offspring.' Therefore, since we are the offspring of God, we ought not to think that the Divine nature is like gold or silver or stone, something shaped by art and man's devising. Truly, these times of ignorance God overlooked, but now commands all men everywhere to repent, because He has appointed a day on which He will judge the world in righteousness by the Man whom He has ordained. He has given assurance of this to all by raising Him from the dead,"* (Acts 17:28-31 NKJV). The foundation on which the church is built is Yeshua HaMashiach alone.

This Cherub did not know a very important secret: He wore his beauty on the outside while Yeshua's beauty was on the inside. The day would come when Abba Father would reveal this awesome life-giving resurrecting and all powerful secret, which was hidden from this fallen Cherub. Eden was not the end for man, it was only the beginning! This once glorified being would see to the crucifixion of Yeshua Jesus because he thought if Yeshua died, the life changing Word would also perish with Him. He gloated for three days believing he was victorious in killing the Son of God, but on the third day this diabolical enemy of Yeshua Jesus and all of mankind received the shock of his life. Yeshua HaMashiach's Spirit from the Father set hell ablaze with His power and glory, thereby stripping our chief enemy of his authority by retrieving the keys of hell and death from him (Revelation 1:18). He was dead wrong again! Yeshua laid down His life therefore He had the power to retrieve it (John 10:17-18).

The Word of God is like a revolving eternal wheel, which the LORD God watches over. The shed blood of Yeshua Jesus broke

41

down the middle wall of separation between GOD and man that was severed in Eden, and restored communication with us Spirit to spirit (John 4:23-24). Yeshua HaMashiach shed His blood as Abba Father planned before He created the fallen Cherub and by His blood Yeshua Jesus won the battle at Calvary for all mankind. It was not Yeshua's outward appearance that won the battle, but that which was on the inside of Him; the life giving, resurrecting power of GOD's Holy Spirit!

Yeshua placed hell and death under His feet by what He possessed on the inside. Yeshua's blood made the difference! It ended animal sacrifices, being the Lamb of God slain before the foundation of the world (John 1:29; 1 John 3:5; Revelation 1:18). This disgraced Cherub was created as a spiritual being and he did not know Abba Father's plan for all, which was the sacrifice of His Son Yeshua, the Word, the Anointed One and our Redeemer. This fallen Cherub now seeks to use mankind to create his own kingdom made up of fallen ones. He failed at overthrowing the Kingdom of God once before, and will be defeated a second time along with those whom he employs to wage war against Israel and the Saints.

The end prepared for Satan and his deceived servants will be one of destruction and the residue of their remains will be ashes upon the earth. Revelation 12:7-11 and 19:19-20 is a message of hope for the children of God: "*And there was war in heaven: Michael and his angels fought against the dragon; and the dragon fought and his angels, and prevailed not; neither was their place found any more in heaven. And the great dragon was cast out, that old serpent, called the Devil, and Satan, which deceiveth the whole world: he was cast out into the earth, and his angels were cast out with him. And I heard a loud voice saying in heaven, Now is come salvation, and strength, and the kingdom of our God, and the power of His Christ: for the accuser of our brethren is cast down, which accused them before our God day and night. And they overcame him by the blood of the Lamb, and by the word of their testimony; and they loved not their lives unto the death. . . . And I saw the beast, and the kings of the earth, and their armies, gathered to make war against Him that sat on the horse, and against His army. And the beast was taken, and with him the false prophet that wrought miracles before him, with which he deceived them that had received the mark of the beast, and them that worshiped his image. These both were cast alive in a lake of fire burning with brimstone."* Yeshua Jesus warns that those who save their life will lose it and those who lose their life for Him, their life would be restored (Matthew 16:25). Do not be afraid of death; it is not the way we die that matters to the Lord, but the life we live! To be absent from the body is to be present with the Lord (2 Corinthians 5:8). Life is short but eternity ís forever, a place devoid of a second chance to repent.

Verses 20-23

"And say, Thus saith the Lord God; Behold, I am against thee O Zidon; and I will be glorified in the midst of thee: and they shall know that I am the LORD, when I shall have executed judgments in her, and shall be sanctified in her. For I will send into her pestilence and blood into her streets; and the wounded shall be judged in the midst of her by the sword upon her on every side; and they shall know that I am the LORD."

It was now time for Tyre's Phoenician sister city Zidon (Sidon), to come under the scrutiny of the LORD. This chief city is located approximately twenty-five miles north of Tyrus. The Zidonians were the descendants of the sons of Canaan who settled near the coastland (see Genesis 10:15; 1 Chronicles 1:13). What else do we know about these people and what could they have done to have caused the Lord to rebuke them? The Zidonians were idolaters and the wisest man who ever lived, King Solomon, fell into idolatry by worshipping Ashtoreth their goddess (1 Kings 11:5a), thereby breaking the first of the commandments. In the New Covenant, Ashtoreth is called the queen of heaven, the Virgin Mary, the blessed mother among other names. Ashtoreth is the goddess of war and pornography, and many tribes of Israel participated in the worship of this strange idol. Jeremiah a prophet of God spoke out against such worship by the mouth of the Lord in chapter 44:13-23. Although Israel was rebuked by the prophet, they stubbornly continued to worship Ashtoreth the chief deity of the Zidonians.

The city of Zidon fell under the judgment of Abba Father because they polluted the worship of His people. For their idolatry, the city of Zidon was judged and plagues, war, and carnage overtook them. Israel and Judah were also punished for worshiping the god Ashtoreth. As Yeshua condemns certain cities for their unbelief

He said: *"What sorrow awaits you, Korazin and Bethsaida! For if the miracles I did in you had been done in wicked Tyre and Sidon, their people would have repented of their sins long ago, clothing themselves in burlap and throwing ashes on their heads to show their remorse. I tell you, Tyre and Sidon will be better off on judgment day than you,"* Matthew 11:21-22 NLT (see also Luke 10:13-14). The Lord calls both Tyre and Sidon (Zidon) wicked, yet stating that these cities would have repented of their sins at the demonstration of the power of God through the miracles that He did. People are drawn to signs and wonders, instead of an unshakable faith in God who judges the world of sin. Tyre, Zidon, and its leaders were warned, but their necks were stiff and their hearts hardened in defiance, therefore sealing their own fate.

Verses 24-26

"And there shall be no more a pricking brier unto the house of Israel, nor any grieving thorn of all that are round about them, that despised them; and they shall know that I am the Lord GOD. Thus saith the Lord GOD; when I shall have gathered the house of Israel from the people among whom they are scattered, and shall be sanctified in them in the sight of the heathens, then shall they dwell in their land that I have given to My servant Jacob. And they shall dwell safely therein, and shall build houses, and plant vineyards; yea, they shall dwell with confidence, when I have executed judgments upon all those that despise them round about them; and they shall know that I am the LORD their God."

This prophecy continues to be fulfilled but the time will come however, when this prophecy will finally be laid to rest, as Israel's trusting relationship and covenant with God is permanently established on earth forever. No more will they be uprooted from their land, for in truth and faithfulness the LORD will establish it. Yeshua Jesus will gather the house of Israel from all the regions of the earth where they have been driven, and set them apart as His own special people. Everyone will know that the LORD God Almighty is for Israel and not against them. They will build once again and their territories will be much greater than before.

Israel will be the cup that will be poured out on the earth as a sign Zechariah 12:2 and 10 states: *"Behold, I will make*

Jerusalem a cup of trembling unto all the people round about, when they shall be in the siege both against Judah and against Jerusalem. . . And I will pour upon the house of David, and upon the inhabitants of Jerusalem, the spirit of grace and of supplications: and they shall look upon Me whom they have pierced, and they shall mourn for him, as one mourneth for his only son, and shall be in bitterness for him, as one that is in bitterness for his firstborn." The prophet speaks of a final peace that will come to the land of Israel, as Yeshua Himself shall be the everlasting Prince of Peace who will see to its fulfillment as He spoke of the times when these things will occur in Matthew 24:32-35.

1948 was a special year for the Jews. On May 14th Israel was declared a nation and the repatriation of its natives continues unto this day, as Isaiah 66:5-8 continues to be fulfilled. Abraham said unto the LORD: *"Oh, that Ishmael might live before You!" Then God said: "No, Sarah your wife shall bear you a son, and you shall call his name Isaac; I will establish My covenant with him for an everlasting covenant, and with his descendants after him,"* (Genesis 17:18-19 NKJV). The Lord GOD Elohim made a covenant with Abraham and his descendants from the children of Isaac as a perpetual covenant. Israel's thorn will one day be removed, and all nations of the earth will know that there is a God in Israel for the scepter shall not depart from Judah (Genesis 49:10) and Yeshua, Israel's righteous King, will judge the inhabitants of the earth. The Lord will no longer wink at the blasphemies spewed upon His people; for he who touches Israel, touches the apple of God's eyes (Zechariah 2:8). God's elect must do their part also, by turning from wickedness unto righteousness or suffer the consequences of being cut off and another rewarded with their blessings. All Israel must remember that righteousness exalts a nation but sin is a reproach unto its people, (Proverbs 14:34). The LORD's judgment against sin is the same for both Jews and Gentiles. He will separate for Himself from both groups a remnant that determinedly walk in holiness, justice and truth, which is the embodiment of pure love.

Chapter 29

Verses 1-16

"In the tenth year, in the tenth month, in the twelfth day of the month, the word of the LORD came unto me, saying. Son of man, set thy face against Pharaoh king of Egypt, and prophesy against him, and against all Egypt: speak and say, Thus saith the Lord GOD; Behold, I am against thee, Pharaoh king of Egypt, the great dragon that lieth in the midst of his rivers, which hath said, My river is my own, and I have made it for myself. But I will put hooks in thy jaws, and I will cause the fish of thy rivers to stick unto thy scales, and I will bring thee up out of the midst of thy rivers, and all the fish of thy rivers, shall stick unto thy scales. And I will leave thee thrown into the wilderness, thee and all the fish of thy rivers: thou shalt fall upon the open fields; thou shalt not be brought together, nor gathered: I have given thee for meat to the beast of the field and to the fowls of the heaven. And all the inhabitants of Egypt shall know that I am the LORD, because they have been a staff of reed to the house of Israel. When they took hold of thee by thy hand, thou didst break, and rend all the shoulder: and when they leaned upon thee, thou breakest, and madest all their loins to be at a stand. Therefore thus saith the Lord GOD; Behold, I will bring a sword upon thee, and cut off man and beast out of thee. And the land of Egypt shall be desolate and waste; and they shall know that I am the LORD: because he hath said, the river is mine, and I have made it, Behold, therefore I am against thee, and against thy rivers, and I will make the land of Egypt utterly waste and desolate, from the tower of Syene even unto the border of Ethiopia. No foot of man shall pass through it, nor foot of beast shall pass through it, neither shall it be inhabited forty years. And I will make the land of Egypt desolate in the midst of the countries that are desolate, and her cities among the cities that are laid waste shall be desolate forty years: and I will scatter the Egyptians among the nations, and will disperse them through the countries. Yet thus saith the Lord God; At the end of forty years will I gather the Egyptians from the people whither they were scattered: and I will bring the captivity of Egypt, and will cause them to return into the land of Pathros, into the land of their habitation; and they shall be there a base kingdom. It shall be basest of the kingdoms; neither shall it exalt itself any more above the nations: for I will diminish them, that they shall no more rule over the nations. And it shall be no more the confidence of the house of Israel, which bringeth their iniquity to remembrance, when they shall look after them: but they shall know that I am the Lord GOD."

Pharaoh is called "a great dragon" intimating his craftiness and power of control by intimidation, which he cleverly utilize to dominate other nations. The Egyptian slavery and oppression of God's people now comes up before the LORD to be judged. The next few years in Egypt would be dismal as those whom they depended upon for support in their fight against Israel in the past would abandon them. Egypt's mighty stature would be abased for a season, because a gracious God would save for Himself a remnant, even amongst the Egyptians. These are the words of the prophet Isaiah concerning Egypt 19:1-18 quoting the NLT: "*This message came to me concerning Egypt: Look! The LORD is advancing against Egypt, riding on a swift cloud. The idols of Egypt tremble. The hearts of the Egyptians melt with fear. "I will make Egyptians fight against Egyptians brother against brother, neighbor against neighbor, city against city, province against province. The Egyptians will lose heart, and I will confuse their plans. They will plead with their idols for wisdom and call on spirits, mediums, and those who consult the spirits of the dead. I will hand over Egypt to a hard, cruel master. A fierce king will rule them," says the Lord, the LORD of Heaven's Armies. The waters of the Nile will fail to rise and flood the fields. The riverbed will be parched and dry. The canals of the Nile will dry up, and the streams of Egypt will stink with rotting reeds and rushes. All the greenery along the riverbank and all the crops along the river will dry up and blow away. The fishermen will lament for lack of work. Those who cast hooks into the Nile will groan, and those who use nets will lose heart. There will be no flax for the harvesters, no thread for the weavers. They will be in despair, and all the workers will be sick at heart. What fools are the officials of Zoan! Their best counsel to the king of Egypt is stupid and wrong. Will they boast to Pharaoh of their wisdom? Will they dare brag about all their wise ancestors? Where are your wise counselors, Pharaoh? Let them tell you what God plans, what the LORD of Heaven's Armies is going to do to Egypt. The officials of Zoan are fools, and the officials of Memphis are deluded. The leaders of the people have led Egypt astray. The LORD has sent a spirit of foolishness on them, so all their suggestions are wrong. They cause Egypt to stagger like a drunk in his vomit. There is nothing Egypt can do. All are helpless the head and the tail, the noble palm branch and the lowly reed. In that day the Egyptians will be as weak as women. They will cower in fear beneath the upraised fist of the LORD of Heaven's Armies. Just to speak the name of Israel will terrorize them, for the LORD of Heaven's Armies has laid out His plans against them. In that day five of Egypt's cities will follow the LORD of Heaven's Armies. They will even begin to speak Hebrew, the language of Canaan. One of these cities will be Heliopolis, the city of the Sun."*

Egypt was a dragon in appearance, receiving counsel from others that caused them more harm than good. The LORD declared that He would place hooks in the jaws of Egypt, which meant He would trap the Egyptians with something that would entice them. This they would accept and those who were their allies and conspirators would also be taken in this snare, which would lead to their final defeat. The land would be utterly decimated and the Egyptians left behind would lament over their downfall for a very long time.

The LORD declared the exact location in Egypt where this devastation would occur. This is quite a vast area, extending from the tower of Syene to the border of Ethiopia. If one should travel from modern day Cairo Egypt to Addis Ababa Ethiopia the distance would be approximately fifteen hundred and twenty-nine miles or two thousand four hundred and sixty kilometer, which is a little less than the distance from Maine to Florida. Syene is also known as Aswan and Swenet, located just south of Egypt on the east bank of the river Nile. Presently there is a dam in Aswan built by the Russians which is said to be amongst the largest embankments ever to be built in the world and was completed in 1970. This dam produces hydroelectric power and has an irrigation system designed to prevent flooding because the Nile is subject to overflow during the rainy seasons. This might have been a good economic venture at the time, but in essence, it was counterproductive and markedly decreased silt, a natural fertilizer containing valuable nutrients which flooded the plains. Due to the decreased silt deposits, the fertile agriculture farm lands of Egypt have almost totally disappeared, while their fishing industry and other profitable commerce have steadily been in decline. Will the Aswan High Dam be responsible for Egypt's economic demise forcing its residence to flee the area?

Another factor to be considered that might hinder rather than serve a good purpose, is the construction of the Grand Ethiopian Renaissance Dam which started in April 2011 and is projected to be completed sometime in 2017. What impact will this dam have on the Nile? Will this Dam cause the total collapse of Egypt's agriculture, fishing, linen and cotton industry? The Egypt economy will remain fragile for many years as prophesied but they will bounce back to the surprise of many, which would be a sign and a witness to the neighboring countries that the LORD has fulfilled His Words through His servants the prophets. The desolation of Egypt will last forty years, and in those days the Egyptians will be refugees in countries that will receive them. At the expiration of this allotted time of their chastisement, the Egyptians will return to their homeland being humbled by the mighty hand of the LORD (see Isaiah 19:19-25). Pathros, located in Upper Egypt, will be repopulated and the Egyptians will worship and serve the LORD with His inheritance Israel.

Verses 17-21

"And it came to pass in the seven and twentieth year, in the first month, in the first day of the month, the word of the LORD came unto me, saying, Son of man, Nebuchadnezzar king of Babylon caused his army to serve a great service against Tyrus: every head was made bald, and every shoulder was peeled: yet had he no wages, nor his army, for Tyrus, for the service that he had served against it: Therefore thus saith the Lord GOD; Behold, I will give the land of Egypt unto Nebuchadnezzar king of Babylon; and he shall take her multitude, and take her spoil, and take her prey; and it shall be the wages for his army. I have given him the land of Egypt for his labor wherewith he served against it, because they wrought for Me, saith the Lord GOD. In that day will I cause the horn of the house of Israel to bud

forth, and I will give thee the opening of the mouth in the midst of them; and they shall know that I am the LORD."

Nebuchadnezzar's army routed and totally devastated the city of Tyrus but strangely enough, took nothing of great value from there. His payment for the plunder of Tyrus would come from the siege against the Egyptians and this would be an indictment against them from God as compensation for what they had done to Israel, trampled, yet not utterly destroyed as the LORD had promised, because the horn of the house of Israel would bud forth as prophesied. The horn of the house of Israel speaks of several things; first of all it refers indirectly to power or authority. Next it is the act of submission and total surrender of a people unto God. Now the budding of Israel is a very significant statement, because at an appointed time the Hebrews will delight in honoring Abba Father, which in-turn will bring them in alignment with His divine purpose for their lives. Through their submission, acknowledgement, and surrender, all mankind who call upon the name of the Lord will also be blessed and these harbingers will occur around the tribulation period. Yeshua Jesus made this point quite clear when He said to His disciples: *"Now learn a lesson from the fig tree. When its branches bud and its leaves begin to sprout, you know that summer is near. In the same way, when you see all these things, you can know his return is very near, right at the door,"* (Matthew 24:32-33 NLT, (see also Mark 13:28-29; Luke 21:29-30).

The budding of Israel indicates that summer is right around the corner which will usher in the reign of Yeshua Jesus on earth. The statement in Ezekiel 29:21: *"In that day will I cause the horn of Israel to bud forth, and I will give thee the opening of the mouth in the midst of them; and they shall know that I am the LORD."* The phrase, *"The opening of the mouth in the midst of them,"* is in fact speaking of a place and not referring to the actual mouth, our organ of speech. *"The opening of the mouth in the midst of them,"* points to a holy site where the worship of Abba Father will be central. The word transliterated for "mouth" is the Hebrew **Peh** [6310], among its several meanings, two stands out: the location of a place and the description of a city's entrance. Next in this sentence is the word *"midst of them"* and *"midst"* is **Tawech** [8432], which points to the presence of God among His people as well as His presence within His people. Looking at this portion of verse in its contextual agreement with the remainder of verses, it is understood that this place is none other than the entrance into the city of Jerusalem. Nations will be gathered there and acknowledge the Sovereignty of the LORD. Prior to this, there will be an outpouring of Holy Spirit and many will accept Yeshua Jesus and be partakers in the New Jerusalem.

The Lord spoke these words by the prophet Isaiah: *"For I, the LORD, love justice; I hate robbery and iniquity. In my faithfulness I will reward them and make an everlasting covenant with them. Their descendants will be known among the nations and their offspring among the peoples. All who see them will acknowledge that they are a people the LORD has blessed. . . For as the soil makes the sprout come up and a garden causes seeds to grow, so the Sovereign LORD will make righteousness and praise spring up before all nations,"* (*Isaiah* 61:8, 9 and 11, NIV). We must continue to pray for the peace of Jerusalem, as the prayer of peace will return upon those who love them (see Psalm 122:6).

Chapter 30

Verses 1-12

"The word of the LORD came again unto me, saying, Son of man, prophesy and say, Thus saith the Lord GOD; Howl ye, Woe worth the day! For the day is near, a cloudy day; it shall be the time of the heathen. And the sword shall come upon Egypt, and great pain shall be in Ethiopia, when the slain shall fall in Egypt, and they shall take away her multitude, and her foundations shall be broken down. Ethiopia, and Libya, and Lydia, and all the mingled people of Chub, and the men of the land that is in league, shall fall with them by the sword. Thus saith the LORD; they also that uphold Egypt shall fall; and the pride of her power shall come down: from the tower of Syene shall they fall in it by the sword, saith the Lord GOD. And they shall be desolate in the midst of the countries that are desolate, and her cities shall be in the midst of her cities that are wasted. And they shall know that I am the LORD, when I have set a fire in Egypt, and when all her helpers shall be destroyed. In that day shall messengers go forth from Me in ships to make the careless Ethiopians afraid, and great pain shall come upon them, as in the day of Egypt: for, lo, it cometh. Thus saith the Lord GOD; I will also make the multitude of Egypt to cease by the hand of Nebuchadnezzar king of Babylon. He and his people with him, the terrible of the nations, shall be brought to destroy the land: and they shall draw their swords against Egypt, and fill the land with the slain. And I will make the rivers dry, and sell the land into the hand of the wicked: and I will make the land waste, and all that is therein, by the hand of strangers: I the LORD have spoken it."

Ezekiel now prophesied of a time in the not so distant future when there will be mourning for the dead in Egypt. This prophecy appears to take on a dual interpretation. First of all this oracle is dealing with Egypt as a nation and secondly, it symbolically represents a country whose mindset is a mirror image of Egypt and therefore is said to be supernaturally influenced by the spirit of Egypt. This is a land of great commerce that was made exceedingly rich by the blood and sweat of its citizens and laborers. It is a place of an invisible demarcation which is built upon a financial class structure. The destruction of this nation will have far reaching effects and the cry of its people will be broadcasted beyond its borders. The hand of the LORD is very patient but when He declares judgment, only true repentance will avert His decree. If this nation does not repent, then it, along with its allies, will experience great distress due to the domino effect that its destruction will have upon them. During ancient times Egypt was a refuge during the great dearth, much as symbolic Egypt is for many in these last days. This land is well known for their art, architecture, well bred horses and fast means of transportation.

In the days of Solomon, he transacted business with the king of Egypt. Following his death Shishak became king of Egypt's and he raided the temple in Jerusalem. 2 Chronicles 12:2-9 states: "*Because they had been* unfaithful to the LORD *Shishak king of Egypt attacked Jerusalem in the fifth year of, King Rehoboam. With twelve hundred chariots and sixty thousand horsemen and the innumerable troops of Libyans, Sukkites and Cushites that came with him from Egypt, he captured the fortified cities of Judah and came as far as Jerusalem. Then the prophet Shemaiah came to Rehoboam and to the leaders of Judah who had assembled in Jerusalem for fear of Shishak, and he said to them, "This is what the LORD says, 'You have abandoned Me; therefore, I now abandon you to Shishak.'" The leaders of Israel and the king humbled themselves and said, "The LORD is just." When the LORD saw that they humbled themselves, this word of the LORD came to Shemaiah: "Since they have humbled themselves, I will not destroy them but will soon give them deliverance. My wrath will not be poured out on Jerusalem through Shishak. They will, however, become subject to him, so that they may learn the difference between serving Me and serving the kings of other lands." When Shishak king of Egypt attacked Jerusalem, he carried off the treasures of the temple of the LORD and the treasures of the royal palace. He took everything, including the gold shields Solomon had made*" (NIV (see also 1 kings 14:25-26)). This was an extremely valuable heist for Egypt, but little did they know that it would become a curse unto their land and the nations that joined in this raid.

Israel is roughly the size of the State of New Jersey, but the truth behind her persecution is not all about religion. The real reason for Israel's hate is stirred by their very large cache of valuable natural resources, the source of their wealth and independence; this is the hook that has baited many nations for centuries. Confederates with Egypt will be Libya and Lydia (present day Ludd). A mixed people identified as Chub or Kub will also be in cahoots with Egypt. With the mention of Chub (Kub), another mystery unfolds as the LORD tells us something that will occur in these last days.

First of all there is a place located in Cairo Egypt called by its full name, Kafr el-Kafr Kub Umaya. Secondly, and of much greater significance, is the fact that there is a type of mobile air-to-sea missiles defense system built by the Russians that is ironically named Kub. This mobile missile system has been used in several wars including the Yom Kippur war of 1973, the Chadian Civil wars, the Iran-Iraq war, the Lebanon war of 1982, the Gulf war and also the Yugoslav wars of 1991-99. Could this symbolically be describing Ezekiel 30:5 which states: *"Ethiopia, and Libya, and Lydia, and all the mingled people of Chub, and the men of the land that is in league, shall fall with them by the sword."* This verse states that the nations allied with Egypt will fall by the sword. The word *"sword"* used in this verse is the Hebrew **Cherev** [2719] transliterated "weapon!"

Ethiopia and Syene also known as Aswan or Swenet, located near the east bank of the river Nile and a few other nations of lesser importance will also be allies in this conspiracy and they will be punished also. Psalm 7:11-16 states: *"God is a just judge, and God is angry with the wicked every day. If he does not turn back, He will sharpen His sword; He bends His bow and makes it ready. He also prepares for Himself instruments of death; He makes arrows into fiery shafts. Behold the wicked brings forth iniquity; yes he conceives trouble and brings forth falsehood. He made a pit and dug it out, and has fallen into the ditch which he made. His trouble shall return upon his own head, and his violent dealings shall come down on his own crown"* (NKJV). The Word of God stands firm throughout eternity; it never fails, unrepentant nations will be judged.

In Ezekiel 30:6, "Migdol," was mentioned in versions such as the NKJV, NASB, and NIV. The name Migdol could be referring to the ancient city of Memphis or symbolically of a place of exaltation. Migdol can also be used figuratively to describe one's pride. During these times of adversities, grief and suffering, the LORD will send forth His messengers into Ethiopia with unfavorable news, being next on His list to experience the same judgment as Egypt.

This prophecy appears to be two-fold with two time lines. The first has already occurred more than twenty-six hundred years ago using lesser war power and the next will occur in the not so distant future using sophisticated modern day technology. The king of Babylon also carries two interpretations; the first was a man who did not worship the God of the Hebrews and the next will be a governmental system and religious ideology. The death toll from this war will be unimaginable. During these times there will be a severe drought like nothing ever seen on the face of the earth. Its ripple effect will cause rivers to look like deserts, thereby making the invasion by the king of Babylon quite easy. The king of Babylon here speaks of the head of a country along with a conglomeration of nations, bound by an affidavit of death and destruction, not knowing that the LORD God Almighty is drawing them out in the open to punish them Himself. The real estate of the Egyptians, which is symbolic of a prideful imperialistic nation, will then be in the hands of their enemies to do as they please.

Verses 13-19

"Thus saith the Lord GOD; I will also destroy the idols, and I will cause their images to cease out of Noph; and there shall be no more a prince of the land of Egypt: and I will put a fear in the land of Egypt. And I will make Pathros desolate, and will set fire in Zoan, and will execute judgment in No. and I will pour My fury upon Sin, the strength of Egypt; and I will cut off the multitude of No. and I will set fire in Egypt: Sin shall have great pain, and No shall be rent asunder, and Noph shall have distress daily. The young men of Aven and Pibeseth shall fall by the sword: and these cities shall go into captivity. At Tehaphnehes also the day shall be darkened, when I shall break there the yokes of Egypt: and the pomp of her strength shall cease in her: as for her, a cloud shall cover her, and her daughters shall go into captivity. Thus will I execute judgments in Egypt: and they shall know that I am the LORD."

In the ancient world the Egyptians practiced polytheism: Amon and Ra were among their chief deities. The LORD informed Ezekiel that for this reason He judged the following six cities and two towns: Pathros, and Zoan, Sin and Noph, Tehaphnehes and No. Aven was the towns center for the worship of Amon and Ra the sun gods, while the cat goddess was worshiped in the town of Pibeseth. Pathros located in Upper Egypt will lay barren, while Zoan will be burned to the ground. The residents of No will suffer immensely and be scattered abroad. As for Sin which is the might of Egypt, its natural defense will be no match for their invaders. Noph located on the west bank of the Nile River will be under constant duress, while the young men of Aven and Pibeseth, the centers of idolatry will die by the sword. There will be great mourning in these cities and those who were spared by the sword will go into captivity. Jeremiah the prophet previously warned of this coming judgment in 46:1-26. Tehaphnehes also known as Tahpanhes, an Egyptian colony located in the Eastern Delta will be in mourning too. Despair will linger over them, as they, too, will be exiled, therefore breaking the heavy burden which Egypt had become.

Verses 20-26

"And it came to pass in the eleventh year, in the first month, in the seventh day of the month, that the word of the LORD came unto me, saying, Son of man, I have broken the arm of Pharaoh king of Egypt; and, lo, It shall not be bound up to be healed, to put a roller to bind it, to make it strong to hold the sword. Therefore thus saith the Lord GOD; Behold, I am against Pharaoh king of Egypt, and will break his arms, the strong, and that which was broken; and I will cause the sword to fall out of his hand. And I will scatter the Egyptians among the nations, and will disperse them through the countries. And I will strengthen the arms of the king of Babylon, and put My sword in his hand: but I will break Pharaoh's arms, and he shall groan before him with the groaning of a deadly wounded man. But I will strengthen the arms of the king of Babylon, and the arms of Pharaoh shall fall down; and they shall know that I am the LORD, when I shall put My sword into the hand of the king of Babylon, and he shall stretch it out upon the land of Egypt. And I will scatter the Egyptians among the nations, and disperse them among the countries; and they shall know that I am the LORD."

Nineveh a major city of Assyria was warned of the coming judgment of the LORD for their idolatry and many other sins; they repented and were spared (Jonah 3:1-10). On the other hand, Egypt's moral and spiritual decay grew worse after being warned by the prophets of the LORD. Prophets such as Isaiah and Jeremiah warned Egypt, but they did not repent (Isaiah 19:1-16; Jeremiah 46:1-26). Because they stubbornly rejected the warnings of the servants of the LORD, war, pestilences and scattering of the people among the nations were inevitable; the pride of their hearts deceived them and they suffered the consequences of their own actions.

Truth is indeed freedom, and those desiring truth, it is given to them. These commands are not for Israel alone, but for all nations. Reading Exodus 20:1-6 from the NKJV: *"And God spoke all these words, saying, "I am the LORD your God, who brought you out of the land of Egypt, out of the house of bondage. You shall have no other gods before Me. You shall not make for yourselves a carved image and likeness of anything that is in heaven above, or that is in the earth beneath, or that is in the water under the earth; you shall not bow down to them nor serve them. For I, the LORD your God, am a jealous God, visiting the iniquity of the fathers upon the children to the third and fourth generations of those who hate Me, but showing mercy to thousands, to those who love Me and keep My commandments."* There is a set time for the judgment of God to come upon a people. Repentance is not to avoid the consequences of our actions, but to show the LORD that we have truly and sincerely turned from wickedness unto righteousness.

Egypt was warned repeatedly but they ignored them, now the gavel strikes for the last time and the conclusion of the matter needed no further deliberation. Nebuchadnezzar the king of Babylon will now be used by Abba Father to punish Egypt. In other words, this imperialistic system will be toppled by another which is both a religion and a governmental ideology. These are the words of the LORD by the prophet Jeremiah: *"At what instant I shall speak concerning a nation, and concerning a kingdom, to pluck up, and to pull down, and to destroy it; if that nation, against whom I have pronounced, turn from their evil I will repent of the evil that I thought to do unto them"* (Jeremiah 18:7-8). The LORD God has not changed; there is no evil intent in His heart towards mankind. Research the track record of nations that acknowledge the LORD and trust in Him; He prospers that nation and allows them to live in peace. On the other hand, a nation that once served the LORD, who turned from righteousness unto wickedness and stubbornly refuse to declare the Sovereignty of God over its people; the LORD will stir up the heathens to be His finger of rebuke unto them. Before the final crushing of such a nation, many pestilences, earthquakes, fires and natural disasters will overtake it, shaking its economy to the core as a direct and final call from Abba Father for national repentance.

Chapter 31

Verses 1-9

"And it came to pass in the eleventh year, in the third month, in the first day of the month, that the word of the LORD came unto me, saying, Son of man, speak unto Pharaoh king of Egypt, and to his multitude; Whom art thou like in thy greatness? Behold, the Assyrians was a cedar in Lebanon with fair branches, and with a shadowing shroud, and of a high stature; and his top was among the thick boughs. The waters made him great, the deep set him up on high with her rivers running round about his plants, and sent out her little rivers unto all the trees of the field. Therefore his height was exalted above all the trees of the field, and his boughs were multiplied, and his branches became long because of the multitude of waters, when he shot forth. All the fowls of heaven made their nests in his boughs, and under his branches did all of the beast of the field bring forth their young, and under his shadow dwelt all great nations. Thus was he fair in his greatness, in the length of his branches: for his root was by great waters. The cedars of the garden of God could not hide him: the fir trees were not like his boughs, and the chestnut trees were not like his branches; nor any tree in the garden of God was like unto him in his beauty. I have made him fair by the multitude of his branches: so that all the trees of Eden, that were in the garden of God, envied him."

As the moral and spiritual decay of the Egyptians were at all time high, their final judgment was made known to the prophet Ezekiel. Once more the LORD spoke to the prophet about Egypt and their confederacy that was both relative as well as symbolic because the greatness of Egypt was undoubtedly inferior to that of the Assyrians. The ancient capital of Assyria was Nineveh, built by Nimrod the great-grandson of Noah (Genesis 10:1-12; 1 Chronicles 1:8-10). The ruler and people of this great city were warned only once by Jonah and they repented instead of having their city destroyed, (Jonah 1:1-2; 3). Egypt, on the other hand, had been warned several times by the prophets but stubbornly continued in their evil ways, choosing death over life. Assyria, a much mightier nation, was used by the LORD as an example to show the Egyptians the power of repentance, with the intention that they would turn from evil and be spared His judgment.

The LORD compares Assyria to the majestic cedars of Lebanon. This is metaphoric language used to describe the nature of their empire. Here is its literal as well as its symbolic interpretation:

- *The Assyrians were a cedar in Lebanon with fair branches* – the cedars of Lebanon were indigenous to the mountainous regions located in the Mediterranean; they can grow up to 130 feet with the circumference of its trunk being more than 8 feet. Its metaphoric interpretation speaks of pride when referring to its height and its world dominance as related to its circumference.

- *They were a shadowing shroud with their tops among the thick boughs* – the cedar trees were massive and had branches that weighed many tons forming a natural yet dangerous canopy. These massive branches would crash to the ground without any warning, causing great damage or death. The symbolic language speaks of the slyness of Assyria; they defeated their enemies by well-planned but swift attacks, catching their victims at a time when they were unprepared and therefore most vulnerable.

- *The waters made them great and the deep set them up* – located in the mountainous regions of the Mediterranean, these trees grew mightily. "Waters" is symbolically referring to the nations; therefore the importance of Assyria among her allies both near and far. Her success and status however was influenced by the supernatural and powerful principality from the underworld.

- *With her rivers running about his plants . . . little rivers were sent unto all the trees of the field therefore his height was exalted. His boughs multiplied and his branches became long because of the multitude of waters when he shot forth* - Assyria was feared among the nations who pledged their allegiance to joined forces with them during their conquests. Because of the affiliation of these nations with Assyria, the nation remained undefeated, which saw to the growth and expansion of their allied forces as well as their kingdom through fear and intimidation.

- *All the fowls of heaven made their nests in his boughs and under his branches did all the beast of the field bring forth their young and under his shadow dwelt all great nations* – the nations whom the Assyrians defeated were taken into exile and allowed some degree of freedom and self-government. The captives also bore children during this period, thereby increasing the diversity, might, and skill of the Assyrian army.

- *He became great because of the length of his branches for his roots were by great waters* – Assyria became a mighty kingdom because of its conquests aided by its multinational army and allies.

Egypt bore similar traits to Assyria, but to a lesser degree. The LORD poses the question to Egypt: *"Whom art thou like in thy greatness?"* Egypt was a very strong nation, but as mighty as they were, they were no match for the LORD of heaven and earth.

Eden was the genesis of God's plan for mankind but it became a place of envy, rebellion and separation. Mankind's propensity for things that appears desirable; possesses the potential of becoming his or her downfall and this innate tendency of man has not changed. The Word of God tells us: *"To the arrogant I say, 'Boast no more,' and to the wicked, 'Do not lift up your horns. Do not lift your horns against heaven; do not speak with outstretched neck.' " No one from the east or the west or from the dessert can exalt a man. But it is God who judges: He brings one down, he exalts another"* (Psalm 75:4-7 NIV). Pharaoh did not control the universe, God does. Now we see how arrogance and pride seals the fate of a people when they fail to repent. Assyria, which is considered to be greater and more powerful than Egypt repented following Jonah's herald of God's coming judgment, while on the other hand, ignoble Egypt raised its ugly fist in defiance. Using the analogy of the Garden of Eden indicated that this was a far greater place, one that was not built by the hands of men, but by the spoken Word of the Living God, and as mighty as the Assyrians were, they were no match for His creative power. This is what the reference to Eden was all about.

In speaking of Assyria the LORD concluded that with all their splendor and renown, their magnificence was tainted by pride. Ezekiel 31:8 states: "*The cedars in the garden of God could not hide him: the fir trees were not like his boughs, and the chestnut trees were not like his branches; nor any tree in the garden of God was like unto him in his beauty.*" The LORD spoke metaphorically and symbolically of these three trees: the cedar, the fir, and the chestnut. Cedars are strong and powerful, fir tree are tall but noble looking in appearance while chestnut trees are much smaller and is dwarfed by the other two. Before the prophetic call for repentance, Assyria used their power and strength for evil; they were described as being opposite to what these trees symbolized. The Assyrians were selfish and ruthless. They were oppressors and a terror unto the weaker nations.

In Ezekiel 31:9, the LORD goes on to say that all the trees in Eden were jealous of the Assyrians. This was not the type of jealousy that stirred malice or envy. In the Garden of God, jealousy was produced and motivated by pure love, each one fulfilling their designed potential. Within the molecular structure of these trees is the genetic marker to be exactly what they were created to be. Symbolically speaking, the grandeur of the cedar tree, the majesty of the fir tree and the might of the little chestnut is the LORD'S way of reminding all mankind that He is in control. The cedar, fir and chestnut were so spoken into existence by the breath of God with a unique purpose in mind, each doing exactly what they were created to do without jealousy, hatred or pride. There is so much to be learned from the symbolic portrayal of these trees, because they declare our uniqueness. Like a small cog in a wheel, we are created by God to work cohesively, because no matter how small our contribution may seem in the natural, it is of great value in the successful completion of something much more greater than we truly realize.

The characteristics of the cedar, chestnut and fir trees was employed by the LORD to metaphorically and symbolically describe qualities of the Assyrians, that although they were powerful and exalted above the nations, they humbled themselves to a much greater Being. The people of Nineveh became unpretentious on hearing the LORD's rebuke (Jonah 3:4-10) and they repented before Him in fasting and prayer after being warned only once of His impending judgment.

Verses 10-18

"Therefore thus saith the Lord GOD; because thou hast lifted up thyself in height, and he hath shot up his top among the thick boughs, and his heart is lifted up in his height; I have therefore delivered him into the hand of the mighty one of heathen; he shall surely deal with him: I have driven him out for his wickedness. And strangers, the terrible of the nations, have cut him off, and have left him: upon the mountains and in all the valleys his branches are fallen, and his boughs are broken by all the rivers of the land; and all the people of the earth are gone down from his shadow, and have left him. Upon his ruin shall all the fowls of the heaven remain, and all the beasts of the field shall be upon his branches: to the end that none of all the trees by the waters exalt themselves for their height, neither shoot up their top among the thick boughs, neither their trees stand up in all their height, all that drink water: for they are all delivered unto death, to the nether parts of the earth, in the midst of the children of men, with them that go down to the pit. Thus saith the Lord GOD; in the day when he went down to the grave I caused a mourning: I covered the deep for him, and I restrained the floods thereof, and the great waters were stayed: and I caused Lebanon to mourn for him, and all the trees of the field fainted for him. I made the nations to shake at the sound of his fall, when I cast him down to hell with them that descend into the pit: and all the trees of Eden, the choice and best of Lebanon, all that drink water, shall be comforted in the nether parts of the earth. They also went down into hell with him unto them that be slain with the sword; and they that were his arm, that dwelt under the shadow in the midst of the heathen. To whom art thou thus like in glory and in greatness among the trees of Eden? Yet shalt thou be brought down with the trees of Eden unto the nether parts of the earth: thou shalt lie in the midst of the uncircumcised with them that be slain by the sword. This is Pharaoh and all his multitude, saith the Lord GOD."

Egypt's sentence was made known to the prophet Ezekiel using the same metaphorical language as spoken before by the LORD. Although these verses appear at first glance to be referring to the Egyptians, the message was dual in nature incorporating their ruling principality: woe to Egypt, woe to their satanic government. Pride and bondage was the nation's spiritual hallmark and many nations, as well as individuals, came under the influenced of this principality. The fall of Egypt would therefore be a sign to the world that the might of the mighty is only for a season, because the LORD is always in control. Meditate upon Numbers 23:19 applying the NKJV: "*God is not a man, that He should lie, nor a son of man, that He should repent. Has He said, and will He not do? Or has He spoken, and will He not make it good?* For further reading see also 1 Samuels 15:29 and Malachi 3:6.

The ruthlessness of Pharaoh became an opened and welcoming door for an evil principality. Temptation is not sin, but yielding to temptation is! All that was said about the king of Egypt has a spiritual duality of a ruler who operates by the spirit of Satan. The Apostle Paul's address to the Ephesians is true for both Old and New Covenant Ephesians 2:1-3 states: "*And you He made alive who were dead in trespasses and sin, in which you once walked according to the course of this world, according to the prince of the power of the air, the spirit who now works in the sons of disobedience, among whom also we all once conducted ourselves in the lust of our flesh, fulfilling the desires of the flesh and of the mind, and were by nature children of wrath, just as the others*" (NKJV). There are no grey areas when it comes to making choices in the kingdom of God; there are two options and only one is desirable. The decisions that one makes identifies which kingdom he or she wants to be a part of, therefore, this is not forced, but an act of one's own volition."

Egypt had to live with the consequences of their actions; they would be struck down. Never again would they oppress or dominate another nation, because the hand of the Almighty had subdued them, leaving them as refuse which no one wanted because their pride and glory was removed. All these judgments ran parallel to the fate of their evil principality: the prince of darkness. Jude 5-6 applying the NET states: "*Now I desire to remind you, (even though you have been fully informed of these facts once for all) that Jesus, having saving the people out of the land of Egypt, later destroyed those who did not believe. You also know that the angels who did not keep within their proper domain but abandoned their own place of residence, he has kept in eternal chains in utter darkness, locked up for the judgment of the great Day.*" This downfall of Egypt and the kingdom of Satan, their spiritual influence, is an example of the humbling of the proud and rebellious. As the Egyptian monarchy received a final and deadly blow, so will the kingdom of darkness.

In Ezekiel 31:18 the LORD asks the question: "*To whom art thou thus like in glory and in greatness among the trees of Egypt? Yet shalt thou be brought down with the trees of Eden unto the nether parts of the earth...*" This address was to the fallen Cherub, the angels who joined him, as well as Pharaoh King of Egypt. All that contaminated Eden the Paradise of God in the past will be totally destroyed one day. The world dominance of the nation of Egypt as well as its spiritual system will one day come to a crushing end as prophesied. Isaiah 19:2-4 states: "*I will set Egyptians against Egyptians; everyone will fight against his brother, and everyone against his neighbor, city against city, kingdom against kingdom. The spirit of Egypt will fail in its midst; I will destroy their counsel, and they will consult the idols and the charmers, the medium and the sorcerers'. And the Egyptians I will give into the hand of a cruel master, and a fierce king will rule over them.*" The day of the LORD's judgment is at hand. This high and lofty nation will be made low and their secret lovers and diviners will abhor them. For centuries the LORD observed Egypt's progressive drifting from righteousness as well as that of her spiritual counterpart, and wooed them to repent but because of pride, they became more divisive and abused their privileges and power. The blood of those they murdered cried out for justice and the LORD heard.

Chapter 32

Verses 1-16

"And it came to pass in the twelfth year, in the twelfth month, in the first day of the month, that the word of the LORD came unto me, saying, Son of man, take up a lamentation for Pharaoh king of Egypt, and say into him, Thou art like a young lion of the nations and thou art as a whale in the seas: and thou camest forth with thy rivers, and troubledst the waters with thy feet, and fouledst their rivers. Thus saith the Lord GOD; I will therefore spread out My net over thee with a company of My people; and they shall bring thee up in My net. Then will I leave thee upon the land, I will cast thee forth upon the open field, and will cause all the fowls of the heaven to remain upon thee, and I will fill the beast of the whole earth with thee. And I will lay thy flesh upon the mountains, and fill the valleys with thy height. I will also water with thy blood the land wherein thou swimmest, even to the mountains; and the rivers shall be full of thee. And when I shall put thee out, I will cover the heaven, and make the stars thereof dark; I will cover the sun with a cloud, and the moon shall not give her light. All the bright lights of heaven will I make dark over thee, and set darkness upon thy land, saith the Lord GOD. I will also vex the hearts of many people, when I shall bring thy destruction among the nations, into the countries which thou hast not known. Yea, I will make many people amazed at thee, and their kings shall be horribly afraid for thee, when I shall brandish My sword before them; and they shall tremble at every moment, every man for his own life, in the day of thy fall. For thus saith the Lord GOD; the sword of the king of Babylon shall come upon thee. By the swords of the mighty will I cause thy multitude to fall, the terrible of the nations, all of them: and they shall spoil the pomp of Egypt, and all the multitude thereof shall be destroyed. I will destroy also all the beasts thereof from beside the great waters; neither shall the foot of man trouble them any more, nor the hoofs of the beasts trouble them. Then will I make their waters deep, *and cause their rivers to run like oil, saith the Lord GOD. When I shall make the land of Egypt desolate, and the country shall be destitute of that whereof it was full, when I shall smite all them that dwell therein, then shall they know that I am the LORD. This is the lamentation wherewith they shall lament her: the daughters of the nations shall lament her: they shall lament for her, even for Egypt, and for all her multitude, saith the Lord GOD."*

It had now been two years since the LORD began speaking to Ezekiel the prophet, concerning Egypt. In this conversation, the LORD focused on the land and its leader. Pharaoh is here described as a young lion of the nation and this was not at all complimentary because it spoke of the trickery, craftiness and violence found in him. Like a young lion, Pharaoh was a hunter who used his clever but deceptive skills to gained notoriety among those equal to him in social standing, rank and military achievement. Not only did the LORD describe Pharaoh as a young lion, He also likened him symbolically to a whale. Pharaoh was surreptitious; appearing to be peaceful, but beneath that façade he could not be trusted. Like the whale, Pharaoh's sleuths, emissaries, and small army would route their enemies, but they were soon to be outwitted by the master of deception, the king of Babylon.

The Babylonian army would subdue, ravage, enslave, and scatter the Egyptians, therefore liberating those who served Pharaoh out of fear. Things appeared quite dismal for Egypt, but as the LORD had promised, He would save for Himself a remnant from among them, a righteous people living in Egypt that would honor Him. Isaiah 19:22 states: *"The LORD will strike Egypt, striking and then healing them. They will turn to the LORD and he will listen to their prayers and heal them"* (NET). Salvation is free but the wages of sin is death and no one who repents will be rejected by the LORD. Many will grieve over the ill-wind that blows upon Egypt and its Pharaoh, but those who turn from evil to do good, joy comes in the morning.

Verses 17-21

"It came to pass also in the twelfth year, in the fifteenth day of the month, that the word of the LORD came unto me, saying, Son of man, wail for the multitude of Egypt, and cast them down,

even her, and the daughters of the famous nations, unto the nether parts of the earth, with them that go down into the pit. Whom dost thou pass in beauty? Go down, and be thou laid with the uncircumcised. They shall fall in the midst of them that are slain by the sword: she is delivered to the sword: draw her and all her multitudes. The strong among the mighty shall speak to him out of the midst of hell with them that help him: they are gone down, they lie uncircumcised, slain by the sword"

Between chapters twenty-nine to thirty-two, ten years had rolled by since the LORD's attention was cast upon Egypt. This nation is the symbol of both pride and bondage combined to create the womb of suppressions and oppression of the righteous. As for the supernatural principality assigned to the leadership of Egypt; a parallel and final judgment was coming. This evil spiritual kingdom and its intricate network governed by fear, intimidation, and apprehension, is a mirror image of Pharaoh and Egypt that will one day be finally overthrown.

Egypt and her allies are now seen as castaways, their judgment now sealed, and their total and permanent separation from the kingdom of light is made known. Egypt will be among the other leaders who have received their punishment for governing their citizens by employing unnecessary hardship. As circumcision symbolically expresses the righteous values seen in a person or nation, un-circumcision is the opposite (Deuteronomy 30:6; Ezekiel 11:19; 36:26; Romans 2:25-29). The LORD condemns no one, but desires all to be saved (John 3:17; 1 John 1:9). Woven into the book of Ezekiel is the fabric of Yeshua's love, justice and redemption for the Jews and engrafted Gentiles. Any person or nation that turns to God wholeheartedly will receive boundless flow of His mercy, grace and blessings. The warnings received by Pharaoh and his nation went unheeded for centuries and the time was now at hand for justice to be served as the wheat is finally separated from the weed.

Verses 22-30

"Asshur is there and all her company: his graves are about him: all of them slain, fallen by the sword: whose graves are set in the sides of the pit, and her company is round about her grave: all of them slain, fallen by the sword, which caused terror in

the land of the living. There is Elam and all her multitude round about her grave, all of them slain, fallen by the sword, which are gone down uncircumcised into the nether parts of the earth, which caused their terror in the land of the living; yet have they borne their shame with them that go down to the pit. They have set her a bed in the midst of the slain with all her multitude: her graves are round about him: all of them uncircumcised, slain by the sword: though their terror was caused in the land of the living, yet they have borne their shame with them that go down to the pit: he is put in the midst of them that be slain. There is Meshech, Tubal, and all her multitude: her graves are round about him: all of them uncircumcised, slain by the sword, though they caused their terror in the land of the living. And they shall not lie with the mighty that are fallen of the uncircumcised, which are gone down to hell with their weapons of war: and they have laid their swords under their heads, but their iniquities shall be upon their bones, though they were the terror of the mighty in the land of the living. Yea, thou shalt be broken in the midst of the uncircumcised, and shalt lie with them that are slain with the sword. There is Edom, her kings, and all her princes, which with their might are laid by them that were slain by the sword: they shall lie with the uncircumcised, and with them that go down to the pit. There be the princes of the north, all of them, and all the Zidonians, which are gone down with the slain; with their terror they are ashamed of their might; and they lie uncircumcised with them that be slain by the sword, and bear their shame with them that go down to the pit."

The Assyrians are descendants from the tribe of Asshur who was the grandson of Noah, and whose father was Shem (Genesis 10:22). The name however is a transliteration of "Asher," "Assur," and "Ashur" and must not be confused with the eighth son of Jacob (Genesis 30:12-13). Ashur was deified as a god of the Assyrians and they worshiped his image as one possessing military strength, conflict and subjugation, which is the very essence of the distinguishing features of the nation itself. It is like a supernatural shadow that can be described as hand and glove; an evil spiritual force working through the natural to achieve its ultimate purpose. These statements regarding this supernatural governing hierarchy also apply to Elam, Meshech, Tubal, Edom and the Zidonians.

Nations that are in constant conflict with each other are unknowingly influenced by a spiritual entity in the heavenly realm. The fallen angel Satan sets up principalities or dominions over regions to procure his evil plan in a constant attempt to destroy humanity through the perpetuation of agitation, conflict and war. The LORD's warning to these nations and cities was also an address to their supernatural counterpart as chaos can only be perpetrated if there is a willing participating host.

The word Ezekiel received from the LORD expressed that these nations, cities, and their spiritual influence, would receive an everlasting punishment, as they would be condemned by a decree of eternal separation from Abba Father. The final resting place for these nations would be an eternal reminder of the evil choices and convictions they vehemently made. The LORD goes on to say that the nation was surrounded by her company in her grave, which is a metaphorical expression describing the final end of Asshur, the Elamites and the other nations along with their corresponding spiritual kingdoms as stated in Ezekiel 32:22-30.

The ancient Elamites were considered to be a warlike people and Jeremiah the prophet, spoke of their judgment also: "*Early in the reign of King Zedekiah of Judah, the LORD spoke to the prophet Jeremiah about Elam. The LORD rules over all said, "I will kill all the archers of Elam, who are the chief source of her military might. I will cause enemies to blow through Elam from every direction like the winds blowing in from the four quarters of heaven. I will scatter the people of Elam to the four winds. There will not be any nation where the refugees of Elam will not go. I will make the people of Elam terrified of their enemies, who are seeking to kill them. I will vent my fierce anger and bring disaster upon them." says the LORD. "I will send armies chasing after them until I have completely destroyed them. I will establish my sovereignty over Elam. I will destroy their king and their leaders." says the LORD. "Yet in days to come I will reverse Elam's ill fortune" says the LORD"* (49:34-39 NET). Elam and Asshur were both sons of Shem and Josephus a first century scholar, documented in his writings that the Elamites were descendants of Elam (Josephus 1.6.4 (see also 1 Chronicles 1:5, 17; Genesis 10:23). Meshech and Tubal are sons of Japheth, and cousins of Asshur and Elam, therefore the listing of Meshech in the family tree of Shem recorded in 1 Chronicles 1:17 must be viewed as a close relative.

Meshech and Tubal are described as being uncircumcised and are jointly judged, an unrighteous brood, which in the eyes of the LORD was a people not in covenant with Him. Circumcision is the seal of God's covenant with Abraham and in Genesis 17:7-13 the Lord GOD declares: *"And I will establish My covenant between Me and you and your descendants after you in their generations, for an everlasting covenant, to be God to you and your descendants after you. Also I give to you and your descendants after you the land in which you are a stranger, all the land of Canaan, as an everlasting possession; and I will be their God." And God said to Abraham: "As for you, you shall keep My covenant, you and your descendants after you throughout their generations. This is My covenant which you shall keep, between Me and you and your descendants after you: Every male child among you shall be circumcised; and you shall be circumcised in the flesh of your foreskins, and it shall be a sign of the covenant between Me and you. He who is eight days old among you shall be circumcised, every male child in your generations, he who is born in your house or bought with money from any foreigner who is not your descendant. He who is born in your house and he who is brought with money must be circumcised, and My covenant shall be in your flesh for an everlasting covenant"* (NKJV). This covenant was also extended to the descendants of Ishmael and the genetic remnant known as the Gentiles.

Next on God's agenda was the land of Edom. To say: *"There is Edom, her kings, and all her princes"* (Ezekiel 32:29), is once more referring to both the natural and spiritual sovereignty of the nation. This phrase is used when speaking of the spiritual dominion that controls these territories. To say "Her," refers to the nation, while "Him," is in reference to the mastermind behind the mindset of the people, and it can either be spiritual, natural, or a combination of both. The bottom line is a known factor that the choices made in the natural by these nations will affect whether there is peace or unrest.

The LORD GOD will however never compromise His holiness. Leaders of nations who govern its citizens through evil dictates will one day itself be ruled by evil. The LORD will not pardon such violations of righteousness; if they continue without repentance, their final judgment will be harsh. Amos 1:11-12 offers some insight into the warlike and unforgiving nature of Edom: "*Thus says the LORD, "For three transgressions of Edom and for four I will not revoke its punishment, because he pursued his brother with the sword, while he stifled his compassion; his anger also tore continually, and he maintained his fury forever. So I will send fire upon Teman and I will consume the citadels of Bozrah"* (NASB). The Edomites are descendants of Esau the older fraternal twin brother of Jacob (Israel), Genesis 32:24-28.

Edom broke covenant and is now grouped with the uncircumcised. The punishment of Edom was a just reward for their uncompassionate nature towards Israel. Ezekiel 25: 12-14 applying the NET states: "*This is what the sovereign LORD says: 'Edom has taken vengeance against the house of Judah; they have made themselves fully culpable by taking vengeance on them. So that is what the sovereign LORD says: I will stretch out my hand against Edom, and I will kill the people and animals within her, and I will make her desolate; from Teman to Dedan they will die by the sword. I will exact my vengeance upon Edom by the hand of my people Israel. They will carry out in Edom my anger and rage; they will experience my vengeance, declares the sovereign LORD.'*" The Edomites had the choice to break the generational curse of hatred and un-forgiveness but chose not to.

The Word of God spoken by His servants the prophets, is God's own inspired Word being poured out and set in motion. This is the very essence of the foundation of who Abba Father is: without mother or father, not matter, but Spirit, not bound by time, but the creator of it, which makes Him the I Am that I Am. The Bible has stood the test of time and its compilation has never been redacted. When the writings were completed by His ministers, He placed His seal upon it and declared a curse upon those who twisted its interpretation for gain. Revelation 22:19 must be taken for all that its worth: "*And if any man should take away from the words of the book of this prophecy, God shall take away his part out of the book of life, and out of the holy city, and from the things which are written in this book.*" This is a deeply profound statement; a stricter judgment awaits those who knowingly use the Word of God for personal gain. The kingdom of God will never be his or her portion and they will find themselves in the pit, their evil living repaid by dwelling with evil, eternally separated from God.

Ezekiel 32:30 states that all the princes of the north and all Zidonians (Sidonians) will receive a final and deadly blow. The LORD spoke of these nations as being uncircumcised, indicating that they were not included in the covenant between Himself and Abraham. He also states that these nations would be slain by the sword because of their unrighteousness. Again the LORD speaks a word but its understanding and interpretation is far reaching.

The sword represents the weapon by which these nations will be punished. The first is the sword of His judgment: the nation that will be used by His Sovereignty to bring about their downfall. Next, the sword refers to the Word of God that He will judge them by. The Word of God is not only Logos or Rhema, it is a person whose name is Yeshua Jesus, and He will judge these nations: *"In the beginning was the Word, and the Word was with God, and the Word was God. He was in the beginning with God. All things were made through Him, and without Him nothing was made that was made. In Him was life, and the life was the light of men. . . . That which was from the beginning, which we have heard, which we have seen with our eyes, which we have looked upon, and our hands have handled, concerning the Word of life the life was manifested, and we have seen, and bear witness, and declare to you that eternal life which was with the Father and was manifested to us that which we have seen and heard we declare to you, that you also may have fellowship with us; and truly your fellowship is with the Father and with His Son Jesus Christ. And these things were written to you that your joy may be full. This is the message which we have heard from Him and declare to you, that God is light and in Him is no darkness at all"* (John 1:1-4; 1 John 1:1-5 NKJV).

The wicked that rejects God's grace will be rewarded with the fruit of their disgrace. Applying the NET Psalm 11 clearly states; *"In the LORD I have taken shelter. How can you say to me, 'Flee to a mountain like a bird!' For look, the wicked prepare their bows, they put their arrows on the strings, to shoot in the darkness at the morally upright. When the foundations are destroyed, what can the godly accomplish? The LORD is in his holy temple; the LORD'S throne is in heaven. His eyes watch; his eyes examine* all people. The LORD approves of the godly, but He hates the wicked and those who love to do violence. May the LORD rain down burning coals and brimstone on the wicked! A whirlwind is what they deserve! Certainly the LORD is just; he rewards godly deeds; the upright will experience his favor." In these last days the LORD is shining His light with greater intensity than ever before upon His Son and the revelation of the Word of God, which is His sword, separating the circumcised from the uncircumcised.

All the leaders of these nations were described as being uncircumcised who will share the rewards of those who were not in covenant with the God of Abraham, Isaac and Jacob. This will be the end as stated by the LORD in Ezekiel chapter 32 for Elam (Persia), Meshech (Syria), Tubal (Lebanon), and Edom (Jordan). The most likely unidentified princes of the north includes: Turkey, Ukraine and the farthest north from Israel; Russia. These nations will join the Zidonians (Sidonians, Palestinians), in this final judgment. Asshur was first mentioned in this decree by the LORD and presently we see the deflation of the might of this nation which is present day Iraq.

By mentioning all the princes or leaders of the north (Ezekiel 32:30) it would include Ukraine, which borders Russia to the east. This country was once a part of the Soviet Union, before receiving their independence, but it is not known what part they will play in the future as far as their inclusion or involvement in the geo-political arena to destroy Israel. At this moment the religion in Ukraine is predominantly Eastern Orthodox Christianity, officially known as the Orthodox Catholic Church. Will they reject God in the future and fight with their allies against Israel? The future will reveal the answer but be it known, any nation that rejects God will ultimately fall into the hands of its enemies.

Verses 31-32

"Pharaoh shall see them, and shall be comforted over all his multitude, even pharaoh and all his army slain by the sword, saith the Lord GOD. For I have caused My terror in the land of the living: and he shall be laid in the midst of the uncircumcised with them that are slain with the sword, even Pharaoh and all his multitude, saith the Lord GOD."

Pharaoh will also see the other fallen nations in the pit and know that the God of justice is impartial, rewarding everyone for their works, whether good or evil. At that moment great regrets will wash over them but it will be too late and their groans of regret will echo in the pit for eternity. Pharaoh's strength was engineered by the spiritual force of the underworld, but now they are faced with the same judgment. Unrighteousness and wickedness are direct opposite of righteousness and justice and the Almighty One takes no pleasure in the death of those who are evil (Ezekiel 18:32; 33:11). There is an appointed time when all these prophesies will be fulfilled. Habakkuk 2 says it all: "*I will stand on my guard post and station myself on the rampart; and I will keep watch to see what He will speak to me, and how I may reply when I am reproved. Then the LORD answered me and said, "Record the vision and inscribe it on tablets, that the one who reads it may run. For the vision is yet for an appointed time; it hastens toward the goal and it will not fail. Though it tarries, wait for it; for it will certainly come, it will not delay. Behold, as for the proud one, his soul is not right within him; but the righteous will live by his faith. Furthermore, wine betrays the haughty man, so that he does not stay home. He enlarges his appetite like Sheol, and he is like death, never satisfied. He also gathers to himself all nations and collects to himself all peoples. Will not all of these take up a taunt song against him, even mockery and insinuations against him and say, 'Woe to him who increases what is not his for how long and makes himself rich with loans?' "Will not your creditors rise up suddenly, and those who collect from you awaken? Indeed, you will become plunder for them. Because you have looted many nations, all the remainder of the peoples will loot you because of human bloodshed and violence done to the land, to the town and all its inhabitants. Woe to him who gets evil gain for his house to put his nest on high, to be delivered from the hand of calamity! You have devised a shameful thing for your house by cutting off many peoples; so you are sinning against yourself. Surely the stone will cry out from the wall, and the rafter will answer it from the framework. Woe to him who builds a city with bloodshed and founds a town with violence! Is it not indeed from the LORD of hosts that peoples toil for fire and nations grow weary for nothing? For the earth will be filled with the knowledge of the glory of the LORD, as the waters cover the sea. Woe to you who make your neighbors drink, who mix in your venom even to make them drunk so as to look on their* nakedness! You will be filled with disgrace rather than honor. Now you yourself drink and expose your own nakedness. The cup of the LORD'S right hand will come around to you, and utter disgrace will come upon your glory. For the violence done in Lebanon will overwhelm you, and the devastation of its beasts by which you terrified them, because of human bloodshed and violence done to the land, to the town and all its inhabitants. What profit is the idol when its maker has carved it, or an image, a teacher of falsehood? For its maker trusts in his own handiwork when he fashions speechless idols. Woe to him who says to a piece of wood, 'Awake!' To a mute stone, 'Arise!' And that is your teacher? Behold, it is overlaid with gold and silver, and there is no breath at all inside it. "But the LORD is in His holy temple. Let all the earth be silent before Him" (NASB). The LORD God will expose all that is done in secret and repay the wicked openly. The nations that curse God's elect will be cursed and the nations that bless God's elect will be blessed. Circumcision is the spiritual covenant and mark of a holy nation; it identifies the elect as being in this world but not of this world. Abba Father in turn identifies with His people, acknowledging their change in spirit, soul, and body and covers them with His peace.

Chapter 33

Verses 1-9

"Again the word of the LORD came unto me, saying, Son of man, speak to the children of thy people, and say unto them, When I bring the sword upon a land, if the people of the land take a man of their coasts, and set him for their watchman: if when he seeth the sword come upon the land, he blow the trumpet, and warn the people; then whosoever heareth the sound of the trumpet, and taketh not warning; if the sword come, and take him away, his blood shall be upon his own head. He heard the sound of the trumpet, and took not warning; his blood shall be upon him. But he that taketh warning shall deliver his soul. But if the watchman see the sword come, and blow not the trumpet, and the people be not warned; if the sword come, and take any person from among them, he is taken away in his iniquity; but his blood will I require at the watchman's hand. So thou, O son of man, I have set thee a watchmen unto the house of Israel; therefore thou shalt hear the word at My mouth and warn them from Me. When I say unto the wicked, O wicked man, thou shalt surely die; if thou dost not speak to warn the wicked from his way, that wicked man shall die in his iniquity; but his blood will I require at thy hand. Nevertheless, if thou warn the wicked of his way to turn from it; if he do not turn from his way, he shall die in his iniquity; but thou hast delivered thy soul."

Once more the LORD re-emphasizes His instructions given to Ezekiel in chapter 3. The office of the prophet or watchman is not one that should be taken lightly, to say, "Thus saith the Lord," when He had not spoken, arises from the emotions or soul and can be very dangerous and misleading as much as the prophecies of a true prophet who polishes his words because he fears retaliation. A true prophet is humble, refrains from drawing attention to him or herself, and like Yeshua, they are grieved over the riotous and unrepentant lifestyle of those around them. This servant, who is called and chosen by the LORD, must make a conscientious effort at all times to remain pure in heart, because prejudice is a hidden and ever present pitfall that ruins his or her credibility and effectiveness.

God speaks through His servants the prophets by the anointing of Holy Spirit, therefore to say "God said" when He had not spoken, is the working of the flesh. The true prophet of God must be without fear and speak the truth in love and without compromise that the condemned might be saved. If the wicked chooses not to repent he or she bears their own reproach. Prophets of God must speak up and speak out against sin just like the prophets of old without regards for their own reputation or safety. If God has truly sent that prophet, He, the LORD, will perform miraculous signs and wonders and if He chooses not to shield them from danger, they will joyfully face the fiery furnace that the blood of the wicked fall directly upon their own heads.

Verses 10-20

"Therefore, O thou son of man, speak unto the house of Israel; Thus ye speak, saying, If our transgressions and our sins be upon us, and we pine away in them, how should we then live? Say unto them, As I live, saith the Lord GOD, I have no pleasure in the death of the wicked; but that the wicked turn from his way and live: turn ye, turn ye from your evil ways; for why will ye die, O house of Israel? Therefore, thou son of man, say unto the children of thy people, The righteousness of the righteous shall not deliver him in the day of his transgression: as for the wickedness of the wicked, he shall not fall thereby in the day that he turneth from his wickedness; neither shall the righteous be able to live for righteousness in the day that he sinneth. When I shall say to the righteous, that he shall surely live; if he trust to his own righteousness, and commit iniquity, all his righteousness shall not be remembered; but for his iniquity that he hath committed, he shall die for it. Again, when I say unto the wicked, Thou shalt surely die; if he turn from his sin, and do that which is lawful and right; if the wicked restore the pledge, give again that he had robbed, walk in the statutes of life, without committing iniquity; he shall surely live, he shall not die. None of his sins that he hath committed shall be mentioned unto him: he hath done that which is lawful and right; he shall surely live. Yet the children of thy people say, The way of the

Lord is not equal: but as for them, their way is not equal. When the righteous turneth from his righteousness, and committeth iniquity, he shall even die thereby. But if the wicked turn from his wickedness, and do that which is lawful and right, he shall live thereby. Yet ye say, The way of the Lord is not equal. O ye house of Israel, I will judge ye every one after his ways."

The justice of God continues to unfold in these verses. Suffering was never His plan for mankind, yet He is blamed for it. The truth of the matter is stated by Yeshua Jesus Himself, *"The thief does not come except to steal, and to kill, and to destroy. I have come that they may have life, and that they may have it more abundantly"*(John 10:10 NKJV). The LORD does not wish to destroy mankind but to redeem them. In John 3:19-21 it is stated: *"And this is the condemnation, that light is come into the world, and men loved darkness rather than light, because their deeds were evil. For every one that doeth evil hateth the light, neither cometh to the light, lest his deeds should be reproved. But he that doeth truth cometh to the light, that his deeds may be made manifest, that they are wrought in God."* We are given the freedom to decide which path to take in life. God does not rejoice over the death of the wicked or of the righteous who turns from his or her righteousness to do evil. In that day that the upright commits evil, and refuses to repent before the LORD, all acts of righteous will be forgotten. On the converse if the wicked acknowledges his or her sins and repent, the Lord will have compassion upon that soul because His mercy and grace is extended to the contrite in heart. 1 John 1:8-9 and Psalm 51:17 applying the NKJV states: *"If we say that we have no sin, we deceive ourselves, and the truth is not in us. If we confess our sins, He is faithful and just to forgive us our sins and to cleanse us from all unrighteousness. . . . The sacrifices of God are a broken spirit, a broken and a contrite heart – these, O God, You will not despise."* As seen here in the Word of God, His justice is unbiased and extended to all.

Verses 21-29

"And it came to pass in the twelfth year of our captivity, in the tenth month, in the fifth day of the month, that one that had escaped out of Jerusalem came unto me, saying, The city is smitten. Now the hand of the LORD was upon me in the evening, afore he that was escaped came; and opened my mouth, until

he came to me in the morning; and my mouth was opened, and I was no more dumb. Then the word of the LORD came unto me, saying, Son of man, they that inhabit those wastes of the land of Israel speak, Abraham was one, and he inherited the land: but we are many; the land is given us for inheritance. Wherefore say unto them, Thus saith the Lord GOD; Ye eat with the blood, and lift up your eyes towards your idols, and shed blood: and shall ye possess the land? Ye stand upon your sword, ye work abomination, and ye defile every one his neighbour's wife: and shall ye possess the land? Say thou thus unto them, Thus saith the Lord GOD; As I live, surely they that are in the wastes shall fall by the sword, and him that is in the open field will I give to the beasts to be devoured, and they that be in the forts and in the caves shall die of the pestilence. For I will lay the land most desolate, and the pomp of her strength shall cease; and the mountains of Israel shall be desolate, that none shall pass through. Then shall they know that I am the LORD, when I have laid the land most desolate because of all their abominations which they have committed."

In the twelfth year of their Babylonian captivity, one of its citizens still living in Jerusalem as a peasant farmer of king Nebuchadnezzar, escaped and found Ezekiel, to express his feeling of pain and dissatisfaction on behalf of those who remained in the city. The day before this fugitive arrived at Ezekiel's doorstep the prophetic anointing of the LORD was strong upon him. The LORD knew the pride that remained in the hearts of the people and the very words of this escapee revealed it. Abraham was indeed the sole person whom God made His covenant to bless the fruit of his loins, but should this blessing give them the right to do as they pleased? Should they take unto themselves wives or husbands of their polytheistic neighbors without fear of the judgment of God? Should they break dietary laws, commit adultery and serve idols? Did the Abrahamic covenant give them the right to practice the abominations of the heathens simply because they were Abraham's descendants and legal heirs to the promise? By God's reply at the mouth of His servant the truth is revealed. The enemies of Israel who lived among them and those far off would afflict them to the point of death, while those left alive would not escape the punishment of God either. Judah would realize that the hand of the LORD was against them because of their abominable sins. Would they be embarrassed to the point of repentance, or would they attempt to justify their sins?

Verses 30-33

"Also, thou son of man, the children of thy people still are talking against thee by the walls and in the doors of the houses, and speak one to another, every one to his brother, saying, Come, I pray you and hear what is the word that commeth forth from the LORD. *And they come unto thee as the people commeth, and they sit before thee as My people, and they hear thy words, but they will not do them: for with their mouth they shew much love, but their heart goes after their covetousness. And, lo, thou art unto them as a very lovely song of one that hath a pleasant voice, and can play well on an instrument: for they hear thy words, but they do them not. And when this commeth to pass, (Lo, it will come,) then shall they know that a prophet hath been among them."*

The hypocrisy of the people was revealed to Ezekiel by the LORD who knows the ways of men. 1 Corinthians 2:10-16 applying the NIV states: *"These are the things God has revealed to us by his Spirit. The Spirit searches all things, even the deep things of God. For who knows a person's thoughts except their own spirit within them? In the same way no one knows the thoughts of God except the Spirit of God. What we have received is not the spirit of the world, but the Spirit who is from God, so that we may understand what God has freely given us. This is what we speak, not in words taught us by human wisdom but in words taught by the Spirit, explaining spiritual realities with Spirit-taught words. The person without the Spirit does not accept the things that come from the Spirit of God but considers them foolishness, and cannot understand them because they are discerned only through the Spirit. The person with the Spirit makes judgments about all things, but such a person is not subject to merely human judgments, for, "Who has known the mind of the Lord so as to instruct him?" But we have the mind of Christ"* The Lord created our bodies with a spirit and a soul, He knows everything about us, nothing is hidden from Him, He is eternally conscious at all times of the deeds of mankind. It is possible for us to deceive others, but we can never deceive the Lord GOD.

The false piousness of the people was exposed. Outwardly they viewed Ezekiel as one who was morally honest, honorable and just, but deep within this was only a cover up of their true motives, and the Spirit who searches the heart of man knew this also. In the end, the proof would be made known as Ezekiel's words are fulfilled. They were only hearers of the words of the Lord, but not doers (James 1:19-27; Jeremiah 1:12; and Isaiah 55:10-11). The oracles of true prophets of God are like a double edge sword that will be fulfilled, because his words are not his own but God breathed; it reproves and it also liberates. The Word of God has the power to cut out the canker of addictive behaviors and it gives hope and a desirable future to all those who believe. It exposes hypocrisy and the empty applauds of the carnally minded. It rebukes the self-righteous who knows it from cover to cover, yet has no proof of its fruit bearing effect in their lives.

Chapter 34

Verses 1-10

"And the word of the LORD came unto me, saying, Son of man, prophesy against the shepherds of Israel, prophesy and say unto them, Thus saith the Lord GOD unto the shepherds; Woe be to the shepherds of Israel that do feed themselves! Should not the shepherds feed the flocks? Ye eat the fat, and ye clothe you with the wool, ye kill them that are fed: but ye feed not the flock. The diseased have ye not strengthened, neither have ye healed that which was sick, neither have ye bound up that which was broken, neither have ye brought again that which was driven away, neither have ye sought that which was lost; but with force and with cruelty ye have ruled them. And they were scattered, because there is no shepherd: and they became meat to all the beasts of the field, when they were scattered. My sheep wondered through all the mountains, and upon every high hill: yea, My flock was scattered upon all the face of the earth, and none did search or seek after them. Therefore, ye shepherds, hear the word of the LORD; As I live, saith the Lord GOD, surely because My flock became a prey and My flock became meat to every beast of the field, because there was no shepherd, neither did My shepherds search for My flock, but the shepherds fed themselves, and fed not My flock; therefore, O ye shepherds, hear the word of the LORD; Thus saith the Lord GOD; Behold, I am against the shepherds; and I will require My flock at their hand, and cause them to cease from feeding the flock; neither shall the shepherds feed themselves anymore; for I will deliver My flock from their mouth, that they may not be meat for them."

These uncaring shepherds were sharply criticized by the LORD for feeding themselves while those around them were in need. They lacked holiness and the more exposure and accolades they received, the farther away they moved from God. They lived for the praises of men not knowing that the author of their faith was about to shake everything around them in an effort to get them back on the highway of righteousness, justice and truth. These tainted shepherds fed upon those they were given to nurture and the little that the people had; plans were constantly being devised to take that too.

The shepherds grew fat, while the flock pined away, clinging to the hope that one day their change would come. These shepherds were not hirelings, they were called to nourish the hungry souls of men, which they did for a short time. Tasting the delicacies of the wealthy, these uncaring shepherds went in pursuit of it for themselves by turning the house of God into a den of thieves, selling that which was freely given to them by the Lord for personal gain. They had no time for the little lambs and sheep, but found all the time for other uncaring shepherds who taught them how to ruthlessly shear the flock. The anointing was intact, their articulation was mesmerizing and the poor little innocent sheep did not know that their shepherd had become corrupt. As the rebuke of the LORD goes unheeded, the shepherd is exposed and the mantle of the LORD which he once wore is removed and given to another servant whom the LORD considers to be more worthy.

Verses 11-16

"For thus saith the Lord GOD; Behold, I, even I, will both search My sheep, and seek them out. As a shepherd seeketh out his flock in the day that he is among his sheep that are scattered; so will I seek out My sheep and will deliver them out of all places where they have been scattered in the cloudy and dark day. And I will bring them out from the people, and gather them from the countries, and will bring them to their own land, and feed them upon the mountains of Israel by the rivers, and in all the inhabited places of the country. I will feed them in a good pasture, and upon the high mountains of Israel shall their fold be: there shall they lie in a good fold, and in a fat pasture shall they feed upon the mountains of Israel. I will feed My flock, and I will cause them to lie down, saith the Lord GOD. I will seek that which was lost, and bring again that which was driven away, and I will bind up that which was broken, and will strengthen that which was sick: but I will destroy the fat and the strong; I will feed them with judgment."

The LORD now gives His people hope for a final re-gathering under His royal banner as the only true Shepherd of His flock is Yeshua Jesus. The LORD uses imagery to describe the times when these things will occur by stating the day will be cloudy and dark, which must be interpreted as the gathering of the Saints during a period of great distress not ever seen on the face of the earth. When darkness covers the whole earth, He will erect the peaceable government of His kingdom under His elect Shepherd as Israel is re-gathered from the places in the earth where they have been scattered. The same God who caused a flood to cover the whole earth, also has the power to cause a massive cloud and accompanying darkness to cover the continents for all to see. Hecklers and abusers of the children of God will witness the LORD gathering His people to feed them upon the mountains of Israel, by the rivers and in all the inhabited places of the country. There the good Shepherd will teach, nurture and establish His offspring in truth and righteousness. Isaiah 49:13-16 offers such hope: "*Sing, O heavens! Be joyful O earth! And break out in singing, O mountains! For the LORD has comforted His people, and will have mercy on His afflicted. But Zion said, "The LORD has forsaken me, and my Lord has forgotten me. Can a woman forget her nursing child, and not have compassion on the son of her womb? Surely they may forget, yet I will not forget you. See, I have inscribed you on the palms of My hands; your walls are continually before Me*" (NKJV). The Lord has not forgotten His people; He will fulfill His promise to restore their joy permanently.

Verses 17-31

"And as for you, O My flock, thus saith the Lord GOD; Behold, I judge between cattle, and between the rams and the he goats. Seemeth it a small thing unto you to have eaten up the good pasture, but ye must tread down with your feet the residue of your pastures? And to have drunk of the deep waters, but ye must foul the residue with your feet? And as for My flock, they eat that which ye have trodden with your feet; and they drink that which ye have fouled with your feet. Therefore thus saith the Lord GOD unto them; Behold, I, even I, will judge between the fat cattle and between the lean cattle. Because ye have trust with side and with shoulder, and pushed all the diseased with your horns, till ye have scattered them abroad; therefore will I

save My flock, and they shall no more be a prey; and I will judge between cattle and cattle. And I will set up one shepherd over them, and he shall feed them, even My servant David; he shall feed them, and he shall be their shepherd. And I the LORD will be their God, and My servant David a prince among them; I the LORD have spoken it. And I will make with them a covenant of peace, and will cause the evil beasts to cease out of the land: and they shall dwell safely in the wilderness, and sleep in the woods. And I will make them and the places round about My hill a blessing; and I will cause the shower to come down in his season; there shall be showers of blessing. And the tree of the field shall yield her fruit, and the earth shall yield her increase, and they shall be safe in their land, and shall know that I am the LORD, when I have broken the bands of their yoke, and delivered them out of the hand of those that served themselves of them. And they shall no more be a prey to the heathen, neither shall the beast of the land devour them; but they shall dwell safely, and none shall make them afraid. And I will raise up for them a plant of renown, and they shall be no more consumed with hunger in the land, neither bear the shame of the heathen any more. Thus shall they know that I the LORD their God am with them, and that they, even the house of Israel, are My people, saith the Lord GOD. And ye My flock of My pasture, are men, and I am your God, saith the Lord GOD."*

As seen throughout the book of Ezekiel the LORD employs symbolic language to get a significant point across. He describes His servants the shepherds as cattle, rams, and he-goats; a mixed brood so to speak. These are the Words of the LORD through His prophet Zechariah: "*My anger is kindled against the shepherds, and I will punish the male goats for the LORD of hosts has visited His flock, the house of Judah, and will make them like His majestic horse in battle*"(10:3 NASB). The use of animal types alludes to certain character traits identified among these shepherds. The LORD will not only judge His servants, but He will also separate them from the Shepherd whom He will appoint to lead the flock into green pastures and that will be His restorative work within them (see Psalm 23). What these shepherds did was a great dishonor to the Father, Yeshua His Son and the ever abiding Holy Spirit. The all-knowing God was keenly aware of the extravagant lifestyle of these shepherds at the expense of the flock, and now compares them with animals: cattle, rams, and he-goats.

In Matthew 25:31-46 the Lord made a profound statement regarding sheep and goats in which He separated them. Great punishment is awaiting these shepherds who are wolves in sheep's clothing. Rams and he-goats are from the family of cattle; therefore, the judgment of the LORD will be against them for their ill-treatment of the sheep. Male species of sheep are called rams, while he-goats are called male goats. The LORD was about to bring judgment upon the male sheep and goats, which is the same as judging between cattle and cattle.

In describing the shepherds as male sheep and goats, the LORD was referring to their character traits and type of leadership. The character of the male sheep (ram), describes those shepherds who demonstrate the qualities that were pleasing to God. The male goat or he-goat on the other hand, is destructive by nature; a hireling spirit is wedged in his soul, and he enjoys the glory and attention of men, instead of leading a humble life before God. He is idolized by those he has bewitched with his charm, eloquence, and charisma; but beneath all this, not a glimmer of anointing can be found because he is driven by an anti-Christ spirit. He sees his calling as a worldly profession rather than the profession of his faith. He lacks devotion and spiritual commitment to do the will of God wholeheartedly because in the back of his mind is the "me" syndrome: "what is in this for me." When we labor in the vineyard of God, the LORD is the one that repays us above that which we can ever imagine. Self-promotion has no place in the kingdom of God, because anything that has to do with "self," promotes self-first.

Goats are independent and destructive, while sheep are co-dependent because they need a shepherd for guidance. Interestingly, if a lamb is raised at birth with goats they tend to sound much like the same and this trait applies to shepherds reared by hirelings. On the converse, it is easier to distinguish between leaders who have come out of congregations of true shepherds because they usually carry the same spiritual mantle, making each group a product of their vineyard or pasture in which they were nurtured. Shepherds compared to goats and rams are identified by their sounds, much like their animal counterpart.

Another difference between goats and sheep is one that is observable: the goat's tail stands erect which is a symbol of pride, while the sheep's tail hangs down which is the mark of humility. In most cases the tail of the sheep is cut off for sanitary reasons and its woolen fleece sheared or shorn, which is symbolic of suffering and sanctification. Yeshua Jesus paid a great price for the sheep. He is described as a good sheep in His suffering and the Lamb of God in His triumph over sin and death for all, (John 1:36; Acts 8:32; 1 Peter 1:19; Revelation 5:6-13; 6:1,16; 7:9-17; 12:11; 13:8; 14:1,4). Matthew 18:11-14 and Isaiah 53:6-7 gives us much to ponder: *"For the Son of Man has come to save that which was lost. "What do you think? If a man has a hundred sheep, and one of them goes astray, does he not leave the ninety-nine and go to the mountains to seek the one that is straying? And if he should find it, assuredly, I say to you, he rejoices more over that sheep than over the ninety-nine that did not go astray. Even so it is not the will of your Father who is in heaven that one of these little ones should perish. . . . All we like sheep have gone astray; we have turned, every one, to his own way; and the LORD has laid on Him the iniquity of us all. He was oppressed and He was afflicted, yet He opened not His mouth; He was led as a lamb to the slaughter, and as a sheep before its shearers is silent, so He opened not His mouth"*(NKJV). Pray for shepherds who have been trapped by an unnatural gravitation towards earthly possession, as an influencing anti-Christ spirit has cast its net of deception over them. This is spiritual warfare in an effort to dismantle the kingdom of God and scatter the sheep and little lambs which are the Saints of God at varying levels of spiritual growth and development.

Pray for hirelings that the scales be removed from their eyes and the truth of God be revealed. Saul who was called Paul following his conversion, once persecuted followers of Yeshua Jesus, yet the Lord transformed his life. The writings of the Pharisee Paul continue to have a profound impact upon humanity; more than any of the twelve disciples who were with Yeshua Jesus during His ministry. Paul spent the remainder of his life completely sold out to the Lord; he suffered greatly, but he kept the faith. The Lord is waiting to do the same for shepherds possessing the nature of cattle and he-goats. He will remove the blinding scales from their eyes that they, too, will cry out in brokenness and humility, "Who art thou Lord?"

Chapter 35

Verses 1-9

"*Moreover the word of the LORD came unto me, saying, Son of man, set thy face against Mount Seir, and prophesy against it, and say unto it, Thus saith the Lord GOD; Behold, O Mount Seir, I am against thee, and I will stretch out mine hand against thee, and will make thee most desolate. I will lay thy cities waste, and thou shalt be desolate, and thou shalt know that I am the LORD. Because thou hast had a perpetual hatred, and hast shed the blood of the children of Israel by force of the sword in the time of their calamity, in the time that their iniquity had an end: therefore, as I live, saith the Lord GOD, I will prepare thee unto blood, and blood shall pursue thee: since thou hast not hated blood, even blood shall pursue thee. Thus will I make Mount Seir most desolate, and cut off from it him that passeth out and him that returneth. And I will fill his mountains with his slain men: in thy hills, and in thy valleys, and in all thy rivers, shall they fall that are slain with the sword. I will make thee perpetual desolations, and thy cities shall not return: and ye shall know that I am the LORD.*"

What did the leaders and inhabitants of Edom commit to have provoked the judgment of God? Other prophets such as Isaiah, Jeremiah and Joel, Amos, and Obadiah also prophesied against Edom. A brief look at Bible history will give us some insight into the Edomites and the reason for such a severe punishment. First of all, it must be understood that Abba Father takes no pleasure in the death of the wicked (Ezekiel 18:30-32; 33:11). The LORD is very patient and gives mankind more time than we justly deserve to repent of our sins. As one seeks the Lord in righteousness on behalf of himself and his progenitors, he or she breaks the curse of the forefathers and prepare a blessed pathway for generations to come.

Edom (modern day Jordan), were settlers of Mount Seir when the LORD spoke of His displeasure with them (Genesis 25:30; 32:3; 36:8, 19). The older fraternal twin brother of Jacob and his descendants occupied this territory. Although the LORD states He is against Mount Seir, the use of the name is employing euphemism and the anger of God was not directed at Mount Seir but the Edomites themselves. Let's see what transpired between the descendants of Esau and Jacob (Israel), to have ignited the judgment of the LORD upon them.

Deuteronomy 2:1-8 and Numbers 20:14-21 applying the NKJV states: "*Then we turned and journeyed into the wilderness of the Way of the Red sea, as the LORD spoke to me, and we skirted Mount Seir for many days. 'And the LORD spoke to me, saying; 'You have skirted this mountain long enough; turn northward. And command the people, saying, "You are about to pass through the territory of your brethren, the descendants of Esau, who live in Seir; and they will be afraid of you. Therefore watch yourselves carefully. Do not meddle with them, for I will not give you any of their land, no, not so much as one footstep, because I have given Mount Seir to Esau as a possession. You shall buy food from them with money, that you may eat; and you shall also buy water from them with money, that you may drink. For the LORD your God has blessed you in all the work of your hand. He knows your trudging through this great wilderness. These forty years the LORD your God has been with you; you have lacked nothing,' " "And when we passed beyond our brethren, the descendants of Esau who dwell in Seir, away from the road of the plain, away from Elath and Ezion Geber, we turned and passed by way of the Wilderness of Moab. . . . Now Moses sent messengers from Kadesh to the king of Edom. "Thus says your brother Israel: 'You know all the hardship that has befallen us, how our fathers went down to Egypt, and we dwelt in Egypt a long time, and the Egyptians afflicted us and our fathers. When we cried out to the LORD, He heard our voice and sent the Angel and brought us up out of Egypt; now here we are in Kadesh, a city on the edge of your border. Please let us pass through your country. We will not pass through fields or vineyards, nor will we drink water from wells; we will go along the Kings Highway; we will not turn aside to the right hand or to the left until we have passed through your territory." Then Edom said to him, "You shall not pass through my land, lest I come out against you with the sword." So the children of Israel* said to him, "We will go by the Highway, and if I or my livestock drink any of your water, then I will pay for it; let me only pass through on foot, nothing more." Then he said, "You shall not pass through." So Edom came out against them with many men and with a strong hand. Thus Edom refused to give Israel passage through his territory; so Israel turned away from him" (see also Judges 11:12-18). Edom, without any risk to their safety, refused Israel passage through their land. Moses and the people received orders to be peaceable with the Edomites and they did. The Edomites however feared Israel and would not allow them to take the short trip through their territory. Without provocation, the Edomites summoned strong men to intimidate and drive Israel away.

In Exodus 3:6 the LORD declares He is the GOD of Abraham, Isaac and Jacob, reemphasizing His covenant with the descendants of this portion of the family tree. In Jeremiah 12:14 He speaks yet again: "*Thus says the LORD: "Against all My evil neighbors who touch the inheritance which I have caused My people Israel to inherit behold, I will pluck them out of their land and pluck out the house of Judah from among them*" (NKJV(see also Joel 3:1-2; Zechariah 2:8). Israel is very special to GOD and those who desired to curse them, Abba Father would place His words in their mouth, thereby changing their cursing into blessings. A good example is Balaam the sorcerer who could not curse Israel because the LORD intervened. Numbers 22:2-6; 24:10-19 applying the NKJV states: "*Now Balak the son of Zippor saw all that Israel had done to the Amorites. And Moab was exceedingly afraid of the people because they were many, and Moab was sick with dread because of the children of Israel. So Moab said to the elders of Midian, "Now this company will lick up everything around us, as an ox licks up the grass of the field." And Balak the son of Zippor was king of the Moabites at the time. Then he sent messengers to Balaam the son of Beor at Pethor, which is near the river in the land of the sons of his people, to call him, saying: "Look, a people has come from Egypt. See, they cover the face of the earth, and are settling next to me! Therefore please come at once, curse this people for me, for they are too mighty for me. Perhaps I shall be able to defeat them and drive them out of the land, for I know that he whom you bless is blessed, and he whom you curse is cursed." . . . Then Balak's anger was aroused against Balaam, and he struck his hands together; and Balak said to Balaam, "I called you to* curse my enemies, and look, you have bountifully blessed them these three times! Now therefore, flee to your place. I said I would greatly honor you, but in fact, the LORD has kept you back from honor." So Balaam said to Balak, "Did I not also speak to your messengers whom you sent to me, saying, 'If Balak were to give me his house full of gold, I could not go beyond the word of the LORD, to do good or bad of my own will. What the LORD says, that I must speak'? "And now indeed, I am going to my people. Come, I will advise you what the people will do to your people in the latter days." So he took up his oracle and said: "The utterance of Balaam son of Beor, and the utterance of the man whose eyes are opened; the utterance of him who hears the words of God, and has the knowledge of the Most High, who sees the vision of the Almighty, who falls down, with eyes wide open: I see Him but not now; I behold Him, but not near; a Star shall come out of Jacob; a Scepter shall rise out of Israel, and batter the brow of Moab, and destroy all the sons of tumult. And Edom shall be a possession; Seir also, his enemies, shall be a possession, while Israel does valiantly. Out of Jacob One shall have dominion, and destroy the remains of the city." Even a sorcerer could not decree curses over Israel, instead, the LORD used the tongue of the wicked to bless His people. In the millennial reign of Yeshua, Israel's Deliverer, Edom and Seir will be the possession of the Jews. The Edomites treated their brethren Israel with contempt and the LORD God would not allow this behavior to go unpunished.

A final look at the sins of Edom takes us to Obadiah the shortest book of the Old Covenant. It explains in much detail the sins of Edom against their brother Israel. The prophet Obadiah wrote this oracle before the times of Jeremiah, and it is stated in 8-15: "Shall I not in that day, saith the LORD, even destroy the wise men out of Edom, and understanding out of the mount of Esau? And thy mighty men, O Teman, shall be dismayed, to the end that every one of the mount of Esau may be cut off by slaughter. For thy violence against thy brother Jacob shame shall cover thee, and thou shalt be cut off for ever. In the day that thou stoodest on the other side, in the day that the strangers carried away captive his forces, and foreigners entered into his gates, and cast lots upon Jerusalem, even thou wast as one of them. But thou shouldest not have looked on the day of thy brother in the day that he became a stranger; neither shouldest thou have rejoiced over the children of Judah in the day of their destruction; neither shouldest thou have spoken proudly in the day of distress. Thou shouldest not have entered into the gate of My people in the day of their calamity; yea, thou shouldest not have looked on their affliction in the day of their calamity, nor have laid hands on their substance in the day of their calamity. Neither shouldest thou have stood in the crossway, to cut off those of his that did escape; neither shouldest though have delivered up those of his that did remain in the day of distress. For the day of the LORD is near upon all the heathen: as thou hast done, it shall be done unto thee: thy reward shall return upon thine own head."

Edom will be punished again for their hatred and evil conniving against their brother Israel. Ezekiel 35:5 applying the NASB states: "Because you have had everlasting enmity and have delivered the sons of Israel to the power of the sword at the time of their calamity, at the time of the punishment of the end, therefore as I live," declares the Lord GOD, "I will give you over to bloodshed, and bloodshed will pursue you; since you have not hated bloodshed, therefore bloodshed will pursue you." Presently, Mount Seir also known as the Shara Range is located near Petra in southern Jordan, but its use in Ezekiel chapter 35 is indeed speaking of the land of Edom which is Jordan itself.

Verses 10-15

"Because thou hast said, These two nations and these two countries shall be mine, and we will possess it; whereas the LORD was there: therefore, as I live, saith the Lord GOD, I will even do according to thine anger, and according to thine envy which thou hast used out of thy hatred against them; and I will make Myself known among them, when I have judged thee. And thou shalt know that I am the LORD, and that I have heard all thy blasphemies which thou hast spoken against the mountains of Israel, saying, They are laid desolate, they are given us to consume. Thus with your mouth ye have boasted against Me, and have multiplied your words against Me: I have heard them. Thus saith the Lord GOD; When the whole earth rejoiceth, I will make thee desolate. As thou didst rejoice at the inheritance of the house of Israel, because it was desolate, so will I do unto thee: thou shalt be desolate, O Mount Seir, and all Idumea, even all of it: and they shall know that I am the LORD."

The Edomites in an attempt to subdue the whole house of Israel, had forgotten one critical piece of information; it was Esau's decision to sell his blessing that was legitimately his being the firstborn son. He chose to satisfy temporary hunger without thinking of its long term effect. This lack of self-control also revealed other character flaws in Esau's personality. He did not possess the essential innate qualities to make a good leader, which was demonstrated by his poor judgment. Esau dishonored the privileges and rights set aside for the firstborn son. By his poor decision he forfeited his blessings and this was an insult to the LORD God. These are the LORD's words to Moses in Exodus 13:2 which states: "*Sanctify unto Me all the firstborn, whatsoever openeth the womb among the children of Israel, both of man and of beast is Mine.*" Esau rejected his blessing and so rejected the privileges that came with it.

Jacob now inherits the blessing and Genesis 27:25-29, 37-44 quoting from the NET ratifies the conclusion of the matter: "*Isaac said, "Bring some of the wild game for me to eat, my son. Then I will bless you." So Jacob brought it to him, and he ate it. He also brought him wine, and Isaac drank. Then his father Isaac said to him, "Come here and kiss me, my son." So Jacob went over and kissed him. When Isaac caught the scent of his clothing, he blessed him, saying, "Yes, my son smells like the scent of an open field which the LORD has blessed. May God give you the dew of the sky and the richness of the earth, and plenty of grain and new wine. May peoples serve you and nations bow down to you. You will be lord over your brothers, and the sons of your mother will bow down to you. May those who curse you be cursed, and those who bless you be blessed."*
. . . Isaac replied to Esau, "Look! I have made him lord over you. I have made all his relatives his servants and provided him with grain and new wine. What is left that I can do for you, my son? Esau said to his father, "Do you have only that one blessing, my father? Bless me too!" Then Esau wept loudly. So his father Isaac said to him, "Indeed, your home will be away from the richness of the earth, and away from the dew of the sky above. You will live by the sword but you will serve your brother. When you grow restless, you will tear off his yoke from your neck." So Esau hated Jacob because of the blessing his father had given to his brother. Esau said privately, "The time of mourning for my father is near; then I will kill my brother Jacob!" When Rebekah heard what her older son Esau had said,

she quickly summoned her younger son Jacob and told him, *"Look, your brother Esau is planning to get revenge by killing you. Now then, my son, do what I say. Run away immediately to my brother Laban in Haran. Live with him for a little while until your brother's rage subsides."* Edom's aggression was not only against their brother Israel, but also against the LORD. The whole house of Israel belongs to God; He is their judge. Because of His covenant with Israel, He takes it upon Himself to either chastise or defend them when the need arose. As Edom (Jordan) planned the desolation of Israel, unknowingly they were preparing the rudiments for their own demise.

Isaiah 41:8-16 stands firm forever as the LORD reminds His people of His covenant with them: *"You, my servant Israel, Jacob whom I have chosen, offspring of Abraham my friend, you whom I am bringing back from the earth's extremities, and have summoned from the remote regions. I told you, you are my servant." I have chosen you and not rejected you. Don't be frightened, for I am your God! I strengthen you yes, I help you – yes, I uphold you with my saving right hand! Look, all who were angry at you will be ashamed and humiliated; your adversaries will be reduced to nothing and perish. When you will look for your opponents, you will not find them; your enemies will be reduced to absolutely nothing. For I am the LORD your God, the one who takes hold of your right hand, who says to you, 'Don't be afraid, I am helping you.' Don't be afraid, despised insignificant Jacob, men of Israel. I am helping you," says the LORD, Your protector, the Holy One of Israel. Look, I am making you like a sharp threshing sledge, new and doubled-edged. You will thresh the mountains and crush them; you will make the hills like straw. You will winnow them and the wind will blow them away; the wind will scatter them. You will rejoice in the LORD; you will boast in the Holy One of Israel"* (NET). Israel is a sign to all the nations of the earth, they are God's prophetic clock. He that blesses Israel will be blessed and he that curses Israel will be cursed and Zion will arise in strength and power under their King and brethren; Yeshua Jesus.

Chapter 36

Verses 1-15

"Also, thou son of man, prophesy unto the mountains of Israel, and say, Ye mountains of Israel, hear the word of the LORD: Thus saith the Lord GOD; Because the enemy hath said against you, Aha even the ancient high places are ours in possession: Therefore prophesy and say, Thus saith the Lord GOD; Because they have made you desolate, and swallowed you up on every side, that ye might be a possession unto the residue of the heathen, and ye are taken up in the lips of talkers, and are an infamy of the people: Therefore, ye mountains of Israel, hear the word of the Lord GOD to the mountains and to the hills, to the rivers, and to the valleys, to the desolate wastes, and to the cities that are forsaken, which became a prey and a derision to the residue of the heathen that are round about; Therefore thus saith the Lord GOD; Surely in the fire of My jealousy have I spoken against the residue of the heathen, and against all Idumea, which have appointed My land into possession with the joy of all their heart, with despiteful minds, to cast it out for a prey. Prophesy therefore concerning the land of Israel, and say unto the mountains, and to the hills, to the rivers and to the valleys, Thus saith the Lord GOD; Behold, I have spoken in My jealousy and in My fury, because ye have borne the shame of the heathen: Therefore thus saith the Lord GOD; I have lifted up Mine hand, Surely the heathen that are about you, they shall bear their shame. But ye, O mountains of Israel, ye shall shoot forth your branches, and yield your fruit to My people of Israel; for they are at hand to come. For, behold, I am for you, and I will turn unto you, and ye shall be tilled and sown: And I will multiply men upon you, all the house of Israel, even all of it: and the cities shall be inhabited, and the wastes shall be builded: And I will multiply upon you man and beast; and they shall increase and bring fruit: and I will settle you after your old estates, and will do better unto you than at your beginnings:

and ye shall know that I am the LORD. *Yea, I will cause men to walk upon you, even My people Israel; and they shall possess thee, and thou shalt be their inheritance, and thou shalt no more henceforth bereave them of men. Thus saith the Lord* GOD; *Because they say unto you, Thou land devourest up men, and hast bereaved the nations; Therefore thou shalt devour men no more, neither bereave thy nations any more, saith the Lord* GOD. *Neither will I cause men to hear in thee the shame of the heathen any more, neither shalt thou bear the reproach of the people any more, neither shalt thou cause thy nations to fall any more, saith the Lord* GOD."

The LORD addresses Ezekiel with His usual use of symbolic language whereby He refers to one thing to explain another. This prophecy was not against literal mountains or hills; neither was it about literal rivers, valleys nor cities. His implicit comparison was in reference to the land, its people and its leaders. There is a subtle and volatile stirring in the Middle East; influenced by a powerful religious spirit of death and destruction, constantly engineering ways to oppress and eventually remove every Jewish trace from that region. The LORD is ever mindful of the plight of Israel, and when all hope to save them seems futile; He will rally His mighty forces and avenge His beloved. Obadiah 15-21 will come to pass in these last days, quoting from the NET: *"For the day of the* LORD *is approaching for all the nations! Just as you have done, so it will be done to you. You will get exactly what your deeds deserve. For just as you have drunk on my holy mountain, so all the nations will drink continually. They will drink, and they will gulp down; they will be as though they had never been. But on Mount Zion there will be a remnant of those who escape, and it will be a holy place once again. The descendants of Jacob will conquer those who had conquered them. The descendants of Jacob will be a fire, and the descendants of Joseph a flame. The descendants of Esau will be like stubble. They will burn them up and devour them. There will not be a single survivor of the descendants of Esau!"* Indeed, the LORD has spoken it. *The people of the Negev will take possession of Esau's mountain, and the people of the Shephelah will take possession of the land of the Philistines. They will also take possession of the territory of Samaria, and the people of Benjamin will take possession of Gilead. The exiles of this fortress of the people of Israel will take possession of what belongs to the people of Canaan, as far as Zarephath, and the exiles of Jerusalem who* are in Sepharad will take possession of the towns of the Negev. Those who have been delivered will go up on Mount Zion in order to rule over Esau's mountain. Then the LORD will reign as King!" For further reading see Jeremiah 31:1-11. History, like most prophecies repeats itself, but the times are at hand when these oracles will be repeated no more, as all of life's drama since God formed man from the dust of the earth comes to a final end. The city of Jerusalem will no longer be a stumbling block to the nations, but a place of refuge and peace.

Verses 16-24

"Moreover the word of the LORD came unto me, saying, Son of man, when the house of Israel dwelt in their own land, they defiled it by their own way and by their doings: their way was before Me as the uncleanness of a removed woman. Wherefore I poured My fury upon them for the blood that they had shed upon the land, and for their idols wherewith they had polluted it: and I scattered them among the heathen, and they were dispersed through the countries: according to their way and according to their doings I judged them. And when they entered unto the heathen, whither they went, they profaned My holy name, when they said to them, These are the people of the LORD, and are gone forth out of His land. But I had pity for Mine holy name, which the house of Israel had profaned among the heathen, whither they went. Therefore say unto the house of Israel, Thus saith the Lord GOD; I do not this for your sake, O house of Israel, but for Mine holy name's sake, which ye have profaned among the heathen, whither ye went. And I will sanctify My great name, which was profaned among the heathen, which ye have profaned in the midst of them; and the heathen shall know that I am the LORD, saith the Lord GOD, when I shall be sanctified in you before their eyes. For I will take you from among the heathen, and gather you out of all countries, and will bring you into your own land."

Abba Father shares His broken heart over Israel with Ezekiel; they had done many abominable things contrary to His teachings which the heathens knew all about, yet they unashamedly confessed to these foreigners and idol worshipers that they belonged to the LORD God. No one cared about the sons of Abraham or about their God, because their lifestyle and confession of faith were opposed in character and purpose as two poles of the same magnetic attraction; making them the target of ongoing insults, mockery and ridicule. Israel neglected to consistently honor their God and so removed themselves spiritually from the one who calls them His beloved and the apple of His eyes. Like a woman who divorces her husband Israel turns their back to their only hope; the LORD their GOD.

The LORD lovingly calls Israel His own people, but this same love was rarely reciprocated to the knowledge of everyone. He was aware from the onset of the relationship that it would be a very difficult task to win the love of His people but He was determined to love them anyway while they, on the other hand kept their covenant relationship only for the security that it offer because they lacked nothing. The LORD knew that Israel would be unfaithful, but remained loyal and would not allow anything to get in His way of protecting them; hoping that the demonstration of His love would soften their wandering hearts. The LORD patiently waits to see if they would abandon their strange lovers and rekindle the dying flame of their affection towards Him, their true and trusted Kingsman Redeemer. The closer the LORD pulled Israel, the more rebellious they became, exploiting the integrity of His grace. Many have failed Him miserably, but in His unbroken covenant with their forefathers, He finds Himself being betrothed to a nation who really doesn't love Him.

Israel profaned the name of the LORD their GOD in the sight of the heathens and He punished them to protect the sanctity of His name. His love however was never far and His covenant never broken. When His punishment ran its course, He would once again be favorable unto them. The house of Israel left Egypt hundreds of years earlier, but the ways of the Egyptians remained like a scourge upon them for generations to come; bad influence surely corrupts good behavior. The repatriation of the children of God to their homeland is ongoing, the times are upon us when the elect of God will rest under the abiding shadow of the ALMIGHTY, never to be plucked up again; the LORD has spoken and He will surely bring it to pass.

Verses 25-38

"*Then I will sprinkle clean water upon you, and ye shall be clean: from all your filthiness, and from all your idols, will I cleanse you. A new heart also will I give you, and a new spirit will I put within you: and I will take away the stony heart out of your flesh, and I will give you a heart of flesh. And I will put My Spirit within you, and cause you to walk in My statutes, and ye shall keep My judgments, and do them. And ye shall dwell in the land that I have given to your fathers; and ye shall be My people, and I will be your God. I will also save you from all your uncleannesses: and I will call for the corn, and will increase it, and lay no famine upon you. And I will multiply the fruit of the tree, and the increase of the field, that ye shall receive no more reproach of famine among the heathen. Then shall ye remember your own evil ways, and your doings that were not good, and shall loathe yourselves in your own sight for your iniquities and for your abominations. Not for your sakes do I this, saith the Lord GOD, be it known unto you: be ashamed and confounded for your own ways, O house of Israel. Thus saith the Lord GOD; In the day that I shall have cleansed you from all your iniquities I will also cause you to dwell in the cities, and the wastes shall be builded. And the desolate land shall be tilled, whereas it lay desolate in the sight of all that pass by. And they shall say, This land that was desolate is become like the Garden of Eden; and the waste and the desolate and ruined cities are become fenced, and are inhabited. Then the heathen that are left round about you shall know that I the LORD builded the ruined places, and plant that that was desolate: I the LORD have spoken it, and I will do it. Thus saith the Lord GOD; I will yet for this be enquired of by the house Israel, to do it for them; I will increase them with men like a flock. As the holy flock, as the flock of Jerusalem in her solemn feasts; so shall the waste cities be filled with flocks of men: and they shall know that I am the LORD."*

As we look towards the future as it relates to the nation of Israel, great events will unfold in the earth that will culminate in their redemption. There will be joyful singing and celebration in Jerusalem, and Judah will praise God in the coming reign of Yeshua Jesus. There will be no more weeping, bondage, and no more turmoil. No more will a dirge be echoed in the land. No more will widows and widowers run in the streets wailing with their dead clutched to their bosoms, because the glory and overshadowing presence of the Prince of Peace will cover the land. These will be times of refreshing and showers of blessing as the dry and parched land gives birth to many crops in abundance. The whole earth will know that Abba Father has blessed His people Israel, and they in turn will be a blessing to Him. They will have a renewed heart, stubbornness and waywardness will be a thing of the past, because the God of Israel is a covenant keeping God who forgives when His elect repents.

Israel will be baptized in the Shekinah glory of her LORD and all her filthiness will be totally washed away never to be remembered. When Israel considers their unfaithfulness, and knowing that the LORD had both forgiven and blessed them to maintain His honor and preserve the integrity of His name, they will weep inconsolably and in brokenness thank Him for His goodness. At the appointed time when these things are fulfilled, all Israel will blossom like the Garden of Eden. Israel's protracted offences against the LORD and their period of bareness will be broken and their blessings heralded around the world. The heathens will recollect the resilience of the people and the might of their GOD, to preserve them from the many attempts of total annihilation throughout the ages. Only then, will these nations become aware that Israel's salvation was not by chance, but by providence. The house of Israel will then re-gather as it were in the days of old during their solemn feasts to offer sacrifices unto the LORD. This sacrifice however, will not be that of a bull or a heifer, but it will be the sacrifice of thanksgiving and praise unto the LORD God, Israel's only hope! Joel 2:21-27 quoting the NKJV states: *"Fear not, O land; be glad and rejoice, for the LORD has done marvelous things! Do not be afraid, you beasts of the field; for the open pastures are springing up, and the trees bears its fruit; the fig tree and the vine yield their strength. Be glad then, you children of Zion, and rejoice in the LORD your God; for He has given you the former rain faithfully, and He will cause the rain to come down for you – the former rain, and the latter rain in the first month. The threshing floors shall be full of wheat, and the vats shall overflow with new wine and oil. "So I will restore to you the years that the swarming locust has eaten, the crawling locust, the consuming locust, and the chewing locust, My great army which I sent among you. You shall eat in plenty and be satisfied, and praise the name of the LORD your God, who has dealt wondrously with you; and My people shall never be put to shame. Then you shall know that I am in the midst of Israel: I am the LORD your God and there is no other. My people shall never be put to shame."* The LORD God will prevail in integrity, love and justice and every word that his prophets have spoken concerning the coming peace of His people will blossom in the earth because it has already been settled in heaven.

Chapter 37

Verses 1-9

"*The hand of the L*ORD *was upon me, and carried me out in the Spirit of the L*ORD*, and set me down in the midst of the valley which was full of bones, and caused me to pass by them round about: and, behold, there were very many in the open valley; and, lo, they were very dry. And He said unto me, Son of man, can these bones live? And I answered, O Lord G*OD*, thou knowest. Again He said unto me, Prophesy upon these bones, and say unto them. O ye dry bones, hear the word of the L*ORD*, Thus saith the Lord G*OD *unto these bones; Behold, I will cause breath to enter into you, and ye shall live: and I will lay sinews upon you, and will bring up flesh upon you, and cover you with skin, and put breath in you, and ye shall live; and ye shall know that I am the L*ORD*. So I prophesied as I was commanded: and as I prophesied, there was a noise, and behold a shaking, and the bones came together, bone to his bone. And when I beheld, lo, the sinews and the flesh came up upon them, and the skin covered them above: but there was no breath in them. Then said He unto me, Prophesy unto the wind, prophesy, son of man, and say to the wind, O breath, and breathe upon these slain, that they may live.*"

The LORD occasionally takes Ezekiel out of his body; the highest form of visionary experience. The Holy Spirit then carries the prophet to a place where the LORD God would show him Israel fragmented and scattered, represented by the scattered bones in the valley. As far as the prophet's eyes could see, there were human bones that were very dry, a symbol of the many centuries that would pass by before Israel would be re-gathered. The LORD strategically placed Ezekiel in the valley where he had a panoramic view of these skeletal remains. There was nothing mysterious about this vision because the LORD was about to explain its meaning.

The LORD carefully chose a valley to reveal the truth about these very dry bones; as there are depths, heights, and widths to this revelation. When we think of bones in this setting, we must reflect on that which makes up a foundation. These were human bones and in the adult there are two hundred and six individual ones. Without bones, all of the sinews and flesh and skin would have nothing to adhere to, no support, no strength and no stability for the body. This is good information, yet the most important fact to note about bones is that they are made up of living cells that manufactures life giving blood in its marrow.

The bones mentioned in Ezekiel were scattered yet not broken. Psalm 34:19-22 applying the NIV states: "*A righteous man may have many troubles, but the LORD delivers him from them all; he protects all his bones, not one of them will be broken. Evil will slay the wicked; the foes of the righteous will be condemned. The LORD redeems his servants; no one who takes refuge in him will be condemned.*" These are powerful and encouraging verses which speak of the LORD'S protection over the righteous. This was a multifaceted vision: bones provide a foundation upon which the body is built and stability maintained; it is also made up of living cells that produces marrow which manufacture blood cells and the bones were scattered and not broken. These facts presented here shows that all twelve tribes of Israel will be re-gathered. Israel is pictured as being the life giving foundation upon which the Gentiles will be a bone graft!

Let's tie in the unbroken bones in the valley with a command given by the LORD in keeping the Passover (Pesach): "*And the LORD said to Moses and Aaron, "This is the ordinance of the Passover: No foreigner shall eat it. But every man's servant who is bought for money, when you have circumcised him, then he may eat it. A sojourner and a hired servant shall not eat it. In one house it shall be eaten; you shall not carry any of the flesh outside the house, nor shall you break one of its bones. All the congregation of Israel shall keep it*" (Exodus 12:43-47 NKJV), (see also Numbers 9:1-14). Yeshua became the enduring Passover sacrifice; Isaiah 53:7; John 1:29; 19:14; 1 Corinthians 5:7. Both the Old and New Covenant testifies of these things; none of His bones were broken (John 19:36). Another word for "break" is the word fracture and apart from its obvious meaning, a fracture can also be rendered as: misuse, to disrupt or destroy.

As God intended, none of Yeshua's bones were fractured and so it is for the whole house of Israel. By their own rebellious ways, Israel was scattered but will be completely restored as we see depicted here in Ezekiel chapter 37. The LORD asked the prophet if the bones could live, then continued by telling him to prophesy to the bones and declare the Word of the LORD unto them. Because of the prophet's fellowship with GOD, he knew that whatever the LORD told him to do would be fulfilled. Why did the LORD tell Ezekiel to prophesy to the bones when He could have spoken the word Himself and the entire valley would instantly be teeming with life? These things are symbolic in nature, but the LORD is informing us that man is the author of chaos, but has the potential of pursuing peace as well. Unity is strength. When man decides to live in genuine peace, then he is harmonizing with his Creator who brings forth life out of every dead situation. Jews from all over the world are still repatriating to Israel and it is people helping people.

Ezekiel's name means "God strengthens," a Levitical priest as well as a prophet of the LORD. Symbolically, Ezekiel represents the coming new man in Yeshua as priest and prophet. Ezekiel also represents all of mankind in a typological setting being the only prophet in the cannon of Scriptures whom the LORD refers to as "son of man;" this He did more than ninety times in the book named after him. In the final millennium, Yeshua the Son of God and Israel's Redeemer who is also called Son of man, our ultimate Prophet and Priest, will oversee the final re-gathering of Jews from all over the world. The LORD now embarks on the foreshadowing of the redemption of the house of Israel and His bondservant Ezekiel was ordained to see and proclaim the coming re-gathering of his scattered, yet unbroken people.

This righteous prophet of God is about to prophesy life and the LORD God is about to perform great signs and wonders before his eyes. Genesis 2:7 states: "*Then the LORD God formed man of dust from the ground, and breathed into his nostrils the breath of life; and man became a living being*" (NASB). By faith, Ezekiel prophesies to the bones scattered in the valley as he was commanded by the LORD, and witnessed the life giving power of the GOD of Israel on display:

- o Breath entered them
- o Sinews were laid upon them

- Flesh covered them
- Skin clothed them
- Breath remained in them
- Life sustained them

Here we see the order of things; breath is what separates the living from the dead. Life must first be given then everything else falls into place. Tough connective tissues known as sinews and tendons attach muscles and bones to the skeletal frame for support. The flesh is the internal protective layer which is necessary to keep the vital internal organs from sustaining injury, while the skin is its outer natural defense. The LORD showed Ezekiel the depth of Israel's suffering throughout the ages and also His unfailing love to preserve them:

- **Bones** – Israel is the true foundation
- **Breath** – separates the living from the dead
- **Sinews** – strength and stability
- **Flesh** – internal protection
- **Skin** – external protection

As Ezekiel prophesies to the bones in the valley, he could hear a tremendous rumbling as he gazed, being transfixed by the awe and wonder of the LORD. The prophet beheld the valley that was once the resting place of dry skeletal remains, too numerous to be counted and clearly understood Moses' writings in Torah, having caught a glimpse of God's creative power firsthand. Bones correctly aligned as sinews and tendons attach themselves to muscles while flesh and skin finally covered them. With apprehension, dismay and bewilderment, Ezekiel observed that they were lifeless. These facts are expressive of the final hours when the wonders that will occur in Israel cannot be attributed to the intervention of man but by the power of God, as He alone has the authority to give the breath of life. In Ezekiel 37:9 the prophet is told to speak to the four winds and breathe upon the slain. Once more the LORD is expressing a secondary message within His command to Ezekiel. Why four winds? In Genesis 2:7 the LORD breathed only once, but now Ezekiel is told to prophesy unto the wind and call forth four winds to breathe upon the slain that they may live.

Here we see the introduction of a fact not previously mentioned that explains Ezekiel 37:3, which states: "*And He said unto* me, Son of man, can these bones live? And I answered, O Lord GOD, thou knowest." There was something unusual in the appearance of the bodies that came forth at GOD's command; not only were they lifeless but they had injuries indicating the cause of death. There are two Hebrew words **Haragh** [2026] and **Heregh** [2027], used substantively in Ezekiel 37:9 for "slain," they both express the act of violence that attributed to one's demise. Ezekiel could now fully understand how the bones got to the valley in the first place. This reversal pattern of putting the pieces together, explains in the present something that had occurred in the past. Ezekiel's answer: "*O Lord GOD, thou knowest,*" could this answer be a weak link in Ezekiel's faith at that time? Could he have doubted the LORD's ability to bring life back into these bones? In 37:8 Ezekiel said "*And when I beheld, lo, the sinews and the flesh came upon them, and the skin covered them above: but there was no breath in them.*" In verses five and six the LORD said He would cause breath to enter into them and they would live. Should the prophet's response: "*O Lord GOD, thou knowest*" be interpreted as a sign of fear, or was it a sign of Ezekiel's resolved faith and understanding that nothing was impossible with God?

Ezekiel did as he was commanded and prophesied to the four winds. This however was not the breath of life, but rather the breath of revival, as Israel is redeemed from the four corners of the earth where they had been dispersed! The first breath that entered them signaled the rebirthing of Israel as a nation. The second breath that came from the four winds was indicative of the breath of revival and redemption, calling wearied Israel to come home. Israel was already fragmented by internal frictions, revolts, hatred, murder and idolatry before they were exiled. Jews would in our lifetime return to the land of Israel by air, land and sea from every region of the earth where they subsequently settled.

Ezekiel's command to prophesy to the four winds was speaking of their repatriation to their own country from the east, the west, the north and the south. These are the words of the Lord about His beloved people Israel by the prophet Isaiah: "*Since you were precious in My sight, you have been honored, and I have loved you; therefore I will give men for you, and people for your life. Fear not, for I am with you; I will bring your descendants from the east, and gather you from the west; I will say to the north,*

'Give them up!' And to the south, 'Do not keep them back!' Bring My sons from afar, and My daughters from the ends of the earth. Everyone who is called by My name, whom I have created for My glory; I have formed him, yes, I have made him" (43:4-7 NKJV, (see also Zachariah chapter 2). The breaths that was breathed upon the slain, was metaphorically describing the re-birth and re-gathering of Israel as one nation, one people; speaking one language under the caring protection of One Savior and LORD.

Verses 10-14

"So I prophesied as He commanded me, and the breath came into them, and they lived and stood up upon their feet, an exceeding great army. Then He said unto me, Son of man, these bones are the whole house of Israel: behold, they say, Our bones are dried, and our hope is lost: we are cut off for our parts. Therefore prophesy and say unto them, Thus saith the Lord GOD; Behold, O My people, I will open your graves, and cause you to come up out of your graves, and bring you into the land of Israel. And ye shall know that I am the LORD, when I have opened your graves, O My people, and brought you up out of your graves, and shall put My Spirit in you, and ye shall live, and I shall place you in your own land: then shall ye know that I the LORD have spoken it, and perform it, saith the LORD."

These verses correspond with Ezekiel 36:24-28; the LORD reiterates His promise to re-gather Israel from all the countries of the earth where they had been scattered; to the land He promised them through an everlasting covenant with Abraham. At this moment, Israel's repatriation is still ongoing as a great number of Jews still lives in the west and other parts of the world. The LORD declared that at an appointed time Israel's sins of the past would be forgiven and their hearts softened as Holy Spirit takes up residence within them. The scales of sin will be severed from their souls and Israel will truly understand the redemptive power of Almighty God towards His elect.

A new revelation of covenant relationship with the Lord will purify them and Israel will finally realize who they are and also to whom they truly belong. With great enthusiasm the people will once again return to the teachings, commands and statutes and rejoice in the God of their salvation, humbling themselves before Him in thanksgiving and rejoicing in the great gratitude of His grace. The prodigal sons of ISRAEL will finally come to their senses, realizing that their Father is King and Ruler of both heaven and earth. They will declare that Abba Father is the Almighty GOD, and He will shout for joy, "You are My people!"

The relationship that the LORD had with His children before the fall of mankind in the Garden of Eden will finally be rekindled and their rest in God will be restored never to be shattered again. Being washed from all their filthiness the betrothed wife Israel, will lovingly embrace their GOD. He has always maintained His integrity even when they had many lovers. He now covers Israel's shame with the veil of His grace and pronounces them ceremonially clean before giving their hands to Yeshua Jesus their Messiah, High Priest and Lord.

The sands of time could not conceal the LORD'S undying love for His people. Most were blinded by religious spirits that they failed to recognize their Messiah as He walked, talked, and did great miracles among them, yet His undying love never waned for His betrothed to reclaim them as His inheritance. They handed Him over to the Gentile Romans, and He suffered the worst and most disgraceful form of death: Crucifixion. Believing Jews in Yeshua Messiah however, were persecuted but the passion and fire ignited within them by their Savior kept burning with even greater intensity.

Some were beheaded, some were fed to the lions, while others were burned at the stake or imprisoned, but they kept the faith knowing that their Redeemer lives. They remembered Yeshua's teaching of the great suffering that would befall Him for their sakes, and recollect His words to them of the hatred they themselves would experience. They would call to mind dining with Him after His resurrection, and peering into the holes in His hands, feet and side; a visible and eternal witness that surely He is the Son of God. Would anyone in their right mind risk death for an imposter? Most knew that they, too, would become a martyr for Yeshua Messiah, but His parting words as He ascended into heaven kept them, knowing that He would one day return. The love, justice and redemptive power of Yeshua Jesus remains as a protective shield over Israel even as they experience many hardships, but in the end Israel's King and legal Heir to the throne of David will woo wondering Israel back into His ever loving arms.

The redeemed sons of God will once again receive life from the spring that flows from Yeshua and His resurrecting power will be sufficient to keep them forever. The same futuristic perfect tense used in Ezekiel 37:5-6 is repeated in verse 14 four times:

- o I shall put My Spirit in you
- o You shall live
- o I shall place you in your own land
- o You shall know that I the LORD have spoken it.

Israel's future is made known. From the beginning of the writings of the Word of God through those whom the LORD had anointed by the resting of Holy Spirit and commissioned as prophetic scribes, to the unfolding of the mysteries written therein; it is clearly proven that these servants could not have documented with such accuracy things to come. Something must be very powerful about the Holy Scriptures as all attempts to destroy it has failed. Man was the hand that penned the Word of God, but it was the mind of God that inspired it. This gives us a very clear understanding why the Word of God has remained indestructible.

To the unbelieving, put aside deistic beliefs for a moment and test the Word of God for yourself and see which other sacred book(s) of other religions parallels the cannon of Scriptures. Which other sacred writings offers a relationship with God? Which other sacred writings have prophetic oracles as the Old and New Covenant that are fulfilled or being fulfilled as we speak? Which other sacred book tells the end from the beginning and the beginning from the end? Abba Father, Yeshua His Son, and the great teacher Holy Spirit are personable, regardless of what is being taught. If one cannot have a relationship with his or her god; he is but a slave doing the biddings of a taskmaster in an endless cycle devoid of love and kinship, fellowship and satisfaction. Psalm 33:12-22 states: "*What joy for the nation whose God is the LORD, whose people he has chosen as his inheritance. The LORD looks down from heaven and sees the whole human race. From his throne he observes all who live on the earth. He made their hearts, so he understands everything they do. The best equip army cannot save a king, nor his great strength enough to save a warrior. Don't count on your warhorse to give you victory for all its strength, it cannot save you. But the LORD watches over those who fear him, those who rely on his unfailing love. He rescues them from death and keeps them alive in times of famine. We put our hope in the LORD. He is our help and our shield. In him our hearts rejoice, for we trust in his holy name. Let your unfailing love surrounds us, LORD, for our hope is in you alone"* (NLT).

The LORD God being the creator of time exists outside the realms of it. He will never allow any evil to enter His Kingdom or reward anyone with eternal life who murders another in the name of religion. The morality and sovereignty of Abba Father would be in question if He requires human beings whom He has created to kill another in the name of religion; this would be a contradiction to His inherent qualities. The Lord God gives us the freewill to choose whom we will serve. He will never order the death of anyone who refuses to worship Him. Being the Supreme Master of heaven and earth, He would simply create us without the capacity for rejecting Him, but because He truly is the LORD GOD Almighty, He gave us a free will to be His sons and not His slaves; this is the epitome of true love. The Lord offers the FREE gift of eternal life not to murderers, but to those who believe and wholly trust in Him. He offers Israel His very own Spirit and a peaceable life with real estate not for killing nor for idolatry or filthiness, but for turning away from every form of sin and unrighteousness.

The Lord God shuns religion, but embraces relationships. War divides but peace brings unity and brotherly love. Righteousness and holiness could not be inspired by the kingdom of darkness, therefore to take the life of another human being in the name of religion is the diabolical working of Satan and his principalities, and his reward is outer darkness and not the kingdom of heaven. All agitations against Israel are inspired by darkness but they will experience a crushing defeat. Israel's historical victories carry the visible and unmistaken signature of God. The times when Israel was greatly outnumbered by their enemies, were the times they had the most miraculous victories!

The Prophet Isaiah spoke of these things, because the nation of Israel is a witness to the world that there is but One GOD, One Savior and Lord; Yeshua Jesus, and One Holy Spirit Ruach

HaKodesh! Applying the NET, Isaiah 43 9-15 states: "*All nations gather together, the peoples assemble. Who among them announced this? Who predicted earlier events for us? Let them produce there witness to testify they were right; let them listen and affirm, 'It is true.' You are my witnesses,*" says the LORD, "*my servant whom I have chosen, so that you may consider and believe in me, and understand that I am he. No god was formed before me, and none will outlive me. I, I am the LORD, and there is no deliverer besides me. I decreed and delivered and proclaimed, and there was no other god among you. You are my witnesses,* "says the LORD, *that I am God. From this day forward I am he; no one can deliver from my power; I will act, and who can prevent it?*" This is what the LORD says, *your protector, the Holy One of Israel:* "*for your sake I send to Babylon and make them all fugitives, turning the Babylonians' joyful shouts into mourning songs. I am the LORD, your Holy One, the one who created Israel, your King.*" Babylon and the Chaldeans metaphorically speak of the nations and their leaders who oppress, enslave, persecuted and killed the people of God, but their final day of reckoning will come.

Verses 15-28

"*The word of the LORD came again unto me, saying, Moreover thou son of man, take the one stick, and write upon it, For Judah, and for the children of Israel his companions: then take another stick, and write upon it, For Joseph, the stick of Ephraim, and for all the house of Israel his companions: and join them one to another into one stick; and they shall become one in thine hand. And when the children of thy people shall speak unto thee, saying, Wilt thou not shew us what thou meanest by these? Say unto them, Thus saith the Lord GOD; Behold, I will take the stick of Joseph, which is in the hand of Ephraim, and the tribes of Israel his fellows, and will put them with him, even with the stick of Judah, and make them one stick, and they shall be one in Mine hand. And the stick whereon thou writest shall be in thine hand before their eyes. And say unto them, Thus saith the Lord GOD; Behold, I will take the children of Israel from among the heathen, whither they be gone, and will gather them on every side, and bring them into their own land: And I will make them one nation in the land upon the mountains of Israel; and one King shall be King to them all: and they shall be no more two nations, neither shall they be divided into two kingdoms any more at all: neither shall they defile themselves any more with their idols, nor with their detestable things, nor with any of their transgressions: but I will save them out of all their dwelling places, wherein they have sinned, and will cleanse them: so shall they be My people, and I will be their God. And David My servant shall be king over them; and they all shall have one Shepherd: they shall also walk in My judgments, and observe My statutes, and do them. And they shall dwell in the land that I have given unto Jacob My servant, wherein your fathers have dwelt; and they shall dwell therein, even they, and their children's children for ever: and My servant David shall be their prince forever. Moreover I will make a covenant of peace with them; it shall be an everlasting covenant with them: and I will place them, and multiply them, and will set My sanctuary in the midst of them for evermore. My tabernacle also shall be with them: yea, I will be their God, and they shall be My people. And the heathen shall know that I the LORD do sanctify Israel, when My sanctuary shall be in the midst of them for evermore."*

The LORD now speaks to Ezekiel using prophetic roll play. The prophet was told to take a piece of stick and inscribe the name of Judah and the children of Israel upon it. Next, he should take another piece and write for Joseph the stick of Ephraim repeating the phrase *and for all the house of Israel his companions,* therefore declaring the reestablishment of Israel as a united nation. Why was Ephraim, Joseph's son included in this annexation with Judah and Israel and what had become of Manasseh his brother? This was a life lesson which demonstrates the importance of decreeing blessings over our children because they will be fulfilled in the same way curses do! As seen here in the reuniting of Israel, a special blessing was ratified upon Ephraim, Joseph's younger son (Genesis 48:14-22). The blessings of Jacob (Israel) were bestowed upon Ephraim therefore Joseph received two portions (Genesis 48:22). Jacob, who was near death, blessed his sons but only Joseph sons were singled out amongst his grandchildren to receive a bonus blessing. Joseph the beloved eleventh son of Jacob was the recipient of a double portion.

As the LORD instructed Ezekiel, he took another piece of stick and inscribed *for Joseph, the stick of Ephraim.* Here we see the unification of the sons of Jacob between Judah, Joseph and Israel and also their companions. Ecclesiastes 4:12 gives a glimpse into the Lord's three-fold binding of the house of Israel, quoting from the NIV the verse states: "*Though one may be overpowered two can defend themselves. A cord of three strands is not quickly broken.*" The fragmented house of Israel will be reestablished again in strength, power and honor.

In Ezekiel 37:16, we see Israel mentioned with the inscription of both Judah and Joseph. Judah was the brother who prevented his other siblings from killing Joseph (Genesis 27:26-27). The three fold binding would not account for all the children of Israel since Joseph was sold to an Egyptian aristocrat. Having one stick uniting Judah and Israel can only be completed with the other stick for Joseph which is Ephraim and the enforcement of the promised double portion blessing. On examining what was next said: "*And for all the house of Israel and his companions,*" the word ALL was mentioned indicating that this was indeed referring to the twelve sons of Israel, with a double portion in Joseph. Israel's companions referred to here, are the Gentile Believers (see Isaiah chapter 14).

United Israel will not be easily subdued; they will prevail as their father Jacob did in the wrestling match with an angel (Genesis 32:22-31). Israel will be reestablished greater in strength against their adversaries. Ephraim was born in Egypt which is symbolic of oppression and bondage. The LORD is revealing here that He will gather the house of Israel and all their Gentile friends as ONE people under the banner of GOD. Micah 4:1-5 states: "*And it will come about in the last days that the mountain of the house of the LORD will be established as the chief of the mountains. It will be raised above the hills, and the peoples will stream to it. Many nations will come and say, "Come and let us go up to the mountain of the LORD and to the house of the God of Jacob, that He may teach us about His ways and that we may walk in His paths." For from Zion will go forth the law, even the word of the LORD from Jerusalem. And He will judge between many peoples and render decisions for mighty, distant nations. Then they will hammer their swords into plowshares and their spears into pruning hooks; nation will not lift up sword against nation, and never again will they train for war. Each of them will sit under his vine and under his fig tree, with no one to make them afraid. For the mouth of the LORD of hosts has spoken*" (NASB). There is but one Israel made up of twelve tribes and their companions are those who have not only stood by them, but have also called upon their God; they, too, will be blessed in Israel's when the tabernacle of God is established forever in Jerusalem.

Chapter 38

Verses 1-3

"And the word of the LORD came unto me, saying, Son of man, set thy face against Gog, the land of Magog, the chief prince of Meshech and Tubal, and prophesy against him and say, Thus saith the Lord GOD; Behold, I am against thee, O Gog, the chief prince of Meshech and Tubal."

Much has been debated regarding these verses. Be it known that Gog is a prefix designated to a leader much like that of President, Prime Minister, Governor or Mayor. He is the elected official for a country which is called by its ancient name Magog. Let's look at a few Scriptures that will reveal the true identity of the man as well as his nation.

○   Genesis 8:1-4

"And God remembered Noah, and every living thing, and all the cattle that was with him in the ark: and God made a wind to pass over the earth, and the waters assuaged [subsided]; the fountains also of the deep and the windows of heaven were stopped, and the rain from heaven was restrained; and the waters returned from off the earth continually: and after the end of the hundred and fifty days the waters were abated. And the ark rested in the seventh month, on the seventeenth day of the month, upon the mountains of Ararat." Here we are told the exact location where the ark came to rest: on the mountains of Ararat located in Turkey, which occupies roughly ninety three percent of Asia Minor. This was the place where Noah, his family and the animals disembarked.

○   Genesis 8:13-19

"And it came to pass in the six hundredth and first year, in the first month, the first day of the month, the waters were dried

up from off the earth: and Noah removed the covering of the ark, and looked, and behold, the face of the ground was dry. And in the second month, on the seven and twentieth day of the month, was the earth dried. And God spake unto Noah, saying, Go forth of the ark, thou, and thy wife, and thy sons, and thy sons' wives with thee. Bring forth with thee every living thing that is with thee, of all flesh, both of fowl, and of cattle, and of every creeping thing that creepeth upon the earth; that they may breed abundantly in the earth, and be fruitful, and multiply upon the earth. And Noah went forth, and his sons, and his wife, and his sons' wives with him: every beast, every creeping thing, and every fowl, and whatsoever creepeth upon the earth, after their kinds, went forth out of the ark."* Here again we see documented proof that Noah, his family and all the animals left the ark in the mountains of Ararat located in modern day Turkey.

o   Genesis 10:1-2 (see also 1 Chronicles 1:5)

"Now these are the generations of the sons of Noah, Shem, Ham, and Japheth and unto them were sons born after the flood. The sons of Japheth; Gomer, and Magog, and Madai, and Javan, and Tubal, and Meshech, and Tiras." Here we are given three of Japheth sons whose names are also mentioned in Ezekiel 38:1-3; Magog, Meshech, and Tubal. Land in ancient times were named after its chief settlers, for example, instead of calling the land sons of Magog, the occupiers would simply name the land Magog. Gog is a reflexive pronoun showing the relationship between the land of Magog and its leader; other examples are King and Prince, Mr. or Mrs. Noah blessed Japheth saying: *"God shall enlarge Japheth, and he shall dwell in the tents of Shem; and Canaan shall be his servant"* (Genesis 9:25-27). Noah could not have cursed his son Ham because God had already blessed him (Genesis 9:1-2); therefore Noah's curse fell upon Ham's youngest son Canaan. Not all of Ham's sons were condemned. The bad omen fell upon Canaan and therefore his descendants; they will initiate the desires of their brethren who are descendants of his uncles Shem and Japheth.

Japheth dwelling in the tents of his brother Shem, speaks of the magnification of the sons of Japheth, who will have greater power and control over both his brothers Shem and Ham. Genesis 9:27 gives another clue: *"God shall enlarge Japheth, and he shall*

dwell in the tents of Shem; and Canaan shall be his servant."
Canaan is indeed Ham's youngest son, whose siblings were Cush (settlers of Northern Sudan); Mizraim (Egypt); and Phut (Libya). Canaan is an extremely vast area extending throughout modern day Israel, Palestine, Syria, Lebanon and Jordon to the west. Did Noah's curse rest upon these nations? Israel is also mentioned as one of the countries making up the land of Canaan but it must be separated; not for any covert bias or prejudice against the other countries, but based on the fact that in the Word of God, the LORD confirmed a blessing upon Israel, therefore superseding Noah's bad omen (Genesis 12:3; 18:18; 22:15-18; 32:24-28; Deuteronomy 33:29; Acts 3:25; Galatians 3:8; Romans 11:26).

The sons of Japheth are powerful leaders; much more than they are given credit and this was so because of their father's blessing. Japheth and his descendants continues to demonstrate how powerful they are over the sons of Shem (Genesis 10:21 list the sons of Shem). Shem is the father of Heber from whom we get the word *Hebrew* or *Semite.* These are all brethren being mentioned here and their differences will never change their DNA. In the genealogy of Shem (Genesis 11:10-32), Abraham is listed as a descendant; and a covenant was ratified between God and Abraham in Genesis 17:15-21. Japheth and his brethren will be a force to be reckoned with in the Middle East; their ties runs much deeper than that of religion or language. They are close relatives and will work as a unified whole to procure their desire which might not necessarily be good.

The sons of Japheth are of one mind and purpose. Gog, from the land of Magog, the chief prince of Meshech and Tubal is referring to a leader of a nation who is exalted among his brothers. This person will be revered because of his great intelligence and military power. His clandestine influence and craftiness will be necessary to aide another close brethren to dominate the geo-political and religious arena worldwide. Gog from the land of Magog will be the mastermind behind this warfare and by his advice, Syria and Lebanon will initiate his orders. This person will prepare the rudiments of war, but his war games will have a deeper and more far reaching effect than his friends or enemies could ever fathom. He will maintain a low profile at first and his non-threatening demeanor will not arouse suspicion or alarm but the plans that he will strategically undertake will have global effect. Although Turkey is the most likely nation where this military leader will arise (see Daniel chapter 11), it will be through the stealth of another leader that Turkey's world dominance will be accomplished. Therefore the most likely country that will be chosen to bring about the coming new world order will be Russia, but they will not be the nation where anti-Christ dogma will be established; this position of preeminence is reserved for Turkey who will undoubtedly be the ones to fan the flame.

Here is a fact worth considering; although these countries are closely tied by bloodline, they are only players. Big games are sponsored by big names; these moguls are the financial supporters whom very few talk about because the focus is always on the players. The same goes for these end time war games. The true mastermind behind these coming catastrophic world events will remain in the background, far from scrutiny or accidental exposure; they are the ones who will ultimately decide who will take center stage as the final superpower for a new world order government subtly appears. In the meantime all inhabitants of this earth will be psychologically and systematically prepared to embrace these coming changes through the covert operation of re-education. As these changes are gradually being put into place, the Middle East will remain volatile as they continue their military and technical support of each other.

Turkey occupies roughly 93% of Asia Minor, while Russia is the largest county in Asia and Europe combined. Turkey provides Syria's opposition coalition with logistic and political backing while Russia is responsible for both their political and arms support. Russia also owns and operates a naval base located in Tartus, Syria's second largest port. Although Russia is not a translation or transliteration of Magog, what is said about their geographical location, using Israel as a point of reference gives us much to consider. Fast-forwarding to Ezekiel 38:14-15 and 39:2 it is written: "*Therefore, son of man, prophesy and say unto Gog, Thus saith the Lord GOD; in that day when My people of Israel dwelleth safely, shalt thou not know it? And <u>thou shalt come from thy place out of the north parts,</u> thou, and many people with thee, all of them riding upon horses, a great company, and a mighty army: . . . And I will turn thee back, and leave but the sixth part of thee, and <u>will cause thee to come up from the north parts</u>, and will bring thee upon the mountains of Israel.*" Countries bordering Israel to the north are Syria and Lebanon, and these are the most likely nations where the attack upon

Israel will commence. Revelation 20:8b applying the NIV states: "*Gog and Magog – to gather them for battle. In number they are like the sand on the seashore.*" This is an exceedingly large army with the same goal in mind. In Revelation 9:16 they are numbered to be two hundred million (200,000,000) a likely coalition of nations and their war games are already underway. Gog from the land Magog will however be punished by the LORD for being the ringleader as these allied forces invades Israel. As payment for their help, Russia will settle for a share of Israel's off shore oil fields as we will see shortly played out like a game of chess. As a note, the Russians are currently the best chess players in the world and are therefore the most likely nation to carry out the plans of these moguls' clandestine war games.

A game of chess consists of:

- o 1 King – He is the weakest but most important in this war game and he never moves into check where he is likely to be captured.

- o 1 Queen – This is the mastermind who exerts great authority over the others. The Queen can move forward, backward, sideways or diagonally as long as she does not move through any pieces that are her own.

- o 2 Rooks – The rook may move liberally forward and sideward; they are the protectors and work harmoniously together.

- o 2 Bishops – These are either light or dark colored and can move as far diagonally. Like the rook, the two bishops work harmoniously and at the same time covers the weaknesses of the others.

- o 2 Knights – The Knights are positioned on two squares going the same direction. They are guaranteed the privileged assignment to make one more move, which is achieved by moving in an "L" shape or a ninety degree pattern. The knights also have the unique ability to move over the other participants in a preemptive stratagem.

- 8 Pawns – There are eight pawns, which move in various directions one square at a time; however, they can only capture while moving forward. If another piece should be directly in front of the pawn this creates a blockade stalling his advance and makes him powerless to gain possession or control. The pawn is also the master of all disguises; if he gets to the opposite side of the board he is promoted and can assume any of the characteristics or role of the others. The pawn is the only piece that can be promoted and dictates the role he will assume, which most likely is the Queen. Surprisingly, the pawn can gain control of another pawn but must do so immediately, otherwise loses the option to do so.

Each piece of the chess game is symbolic of a nation that has an assigned role to play in the end of time great wars. Nations designated the duties of a pawn are the only ones with the ability to assume the title of any of the remaining participants as he so chose. The countries assigned as key pieces on the board, generally move into positions where they can capture another country by landing and overthrowing it. They can also defer to capture or control important nations at their own discretion. There is much more to the game of chess, but the point intended here is to show the purpose and movement of each nation working as a coalition to achieve the same goal. Note also that there is a total of six named pieces, the number assigned to man. One must never underestimate the power of unity. The influential leaders of these nations are aware of the genetic ties that bind them and will collaborate to achieve the desired goal of another. All eyes must now be focused in these coming years on Turkey and Russia, and this presumption is scripturally based. Turkey will reign supreme for a season being the center of anarchy that will consume the whole earth.

There is a city named Pergamum (Pergamos) located in Turkey and in Revelation 2:12-13 there is a startling piece of information in the body of the text spoken by Yeshua Jesus in His address to Believers residing there. Quoting from the NET it is stated: "*To the angel of the church of Pergamum write the following: this is the solemn pronouncement of the one who has the sharp double-edged sword: 'I know where you live – where Satan's throne is. Yet you continue to cling to my name and you have* not denied your faith in me, even in the days of Antipas, my faithful witness, who was killed in your city where Satan lives." Although this is telling us of a past event in the city of Pergamum, history will repeat itself. Yeshua Jesus calls Pergamum which is located in Turkey, "Satan's throne." Turkey will play a key role in upcoming world events which will be more than wars and rumors of war because this is the headquarters of the Russian operation. More will soon be revealed about Turkey and their coming geo-political and world dominance.

Fast forwarding to Ezekiel 38:15 it is said that "they will be riding upon horses;" this is a play on words; the Hebraic root for "riding," can also mean driving a vehicle and the word used for "horses," can be rendered as rapid flight. Based on the Hebraic rendering of these words, the launching attack against Israel will most likely be given from a commanding center located in Turkey [Satan's throne]. Turkey is about five hundred and forty-eight miles or eight hundred and eighty-two kilometers from Israel; while Lebanon, Jordan, Cairo Egypt and Syria are even closer. These could be five of the six pawns (Turkey included) where the strikes on Israel will originate. With the aid of the Russian military, Syria and Lebanon will most likely commence land and air strikes since their borders are closer to Israel. Israel will suffer a major defeat, but because of the LORD's covenant with them, and also to retain the honor of His name, His people will not be completely annihilated. He who stepped in and gave Israel the victory against all odds over their enemies in the wars of the twentieth century will also procure victory for Israel once again. Israel will rally with a few skilled soldiers and win this final battle: not by might, nor by power, but by the supernatural intervention of the LORD of Heaven's mighty hosts!

Verses 4-7

"And I will turn thee back, and put hooks into thy jaws, and I will bring thee forth, and all thine army, horses and horsemen, all of them clothed with all sorts of armor, even a great company with bucklers and shields, all of them handling swords: Persia, Ethiopia, and Libya with them; all of them with shield and helmet. Gomer, and all his bands; the house of Togarmah of the north quarters, and all his bands: and many people with thee. Be thou prepared, and prepare for thyself, thou, and all thy company that are assembled unto thee, and be thou a guard unto them."

129

The Lord now decrees by the mouth of Ezekiel that the plans against Israel will have a surprising unexpected outcome because Israel will gain the upper hand. This will cause internal conflicts amongst their enemies as each one blames the other for being outwitted by the Israeli Defense Force. Russia, Syria, and Lebanon will be crushed, and their allies: Ethiopia [Cush–present day Northern Sudan], Libya [Put], Germany [Gomer], and Turkey [Togarmah] will suffer great casualties also. Germany [Gomer], the oldest son of Japheth is also included in this judgment because the LORD did not forget the holocaust. Greece, France and Spain are also worth mentioning as these settlers are also sons of Japheth and at this moment they are in a state of spiritual and economic decline. It would appear that all seven sons are being judged by the LORD which would override all previous words of blessing by Noah.

Ezekiel 38:4 spoke of "putting hooks into thy jaw**s**," which means to subdue or overcome one; "jaws;" is in its plural form, indicating more than one country will be involved in this plot, and crude oil is the most likely bait that will lure them. Presently, Israel is a technological and scientifically advanced nation with a highly developed agricultural industry ranked among the finest in the world. Oil shale deposits are located all over Israel and its mining will catapult Israel's economy unto the world seen and these events were prophesied thousands of years earlier. More will be said about Israel's oil and natural gas. The plans to destroy Israel will be the mastermind of Russia, but all eyes must focus upon Turkey, as Israel was once a part of the Turkish Empire (Ottoman) during the Diaspora. Israel is like a precious jewel in the desert that Turkey wishes to reclaim at all cost. The first invasion of Israel by allied forces will fail, but their enemies will come against the land a second time and be marginally successful (see Daniel 11).

Deuteronomy 33:13-16, 18-19 and 24-25 are prophetic blessings that we see occurring in the land of Israel. These are Moses words; quoting from the NKJV: "*And of Joseph he said, Blessed of the LORD be his land, for the precious things of heaven, for the dew, and for the deep that coucheth beneath, and for the precious fruits brought forth by the sun, and for the precious things put forth by the moon, and for the chief things of the ancient mountains, and for the precious things of the lasting hills, and for the precious things of the earth and fullness thereof, and for the good will of him that dwelt in the bush: let the blessing come upon the head of Joseph, and upon the top of the head of him that was separated from his brethren. . . . And of Zebulun he said, Rejoice, Zebulun, in thy going out; and, Issachar, in thy tents. They shall call the people unto the mountain; there they shall offer sacrifices of righteousness: for they shall suck of the abundance of the seas, and of treasures hid in the sand. . . . And of Asher he said, Let Asher be blessed with children; let him be acceptable to his brethren, and let him dip his foot in oil. Thy shoes shall be iron and brass; and as thy days, so shall thy strength be"* (see also Genesis 49:13, 14, 20 and 22). These words are being fulfilled as we speak. Israel will someday process natural gas and oil in a vast quantity and the greedy will be hooked. Israel however will not bend or bow to any nation desiring partnership with them during exploration, and their stance will infuriate the covetous who will ignite war to take the oil and natural gas by force, thereby becoming the bait that lures them. It is written in the Holy Scriptures that Asher will *dip his foot in oil*, notice the verse did not say dip his feet in oil; therefore it must be understood that other nations will want drilling rights in Israel as well. This will be a life or death situation, but the LORD God of Israel is truly the rightful owner of this piece of real estate and He will perform great signs and wonders to the quaking of the nations of the earth.

Verses 8-18

"After many days thou shalt be visited: in the latter years thou shalt come into the land that is brought back from the sword, and is gathered out of many people, against the mountains of Israel, which have been always waste: but it is brought forth out of the nations, and they shall dwell safely all of them. Thou shall ascend and come like a storm, thou shalt be like a cloud to cover the land, thou, and all thy bands, and many people with thee. Thus saith the Lord GOD; It shall also come to pass, that at the same time shall things come into thy mind, and thou shalt think an evil thought; and thou shalt say, I will go up to the land of unwalled villages; I will go to them that are at rest, that dwell safely, all of them dwelling without walls, and having neither bars nor gates, to take a spoil, and to take a prey; to turn thine hand upon the desolate places that are now inhabited, and upon the people that are gathered out of the nations, which have gotten cattle and goods, that dwell in the midst of

the land. Sheba, and Dedan, and the merchants of Tarshish, with all the young lions thereof, shall say unto thee, Art thou come to take a spoil? Hast thou gathered thy company to take a prey? To carry away silver and gold, to take away cattle and goods, to take a great spoil? Therefore, son of man, prophesy and say unto Gog, Thus saith the Lord GOD; In that day when My people of Israel dwelleth safely, shalt thou not know it? And thou shalt come from thy place out of the north parts, thou, and many people with thee, all of them riding upon horses, a great company, and a mighty army: and thou shalt come up against My people of Israel, as a cloud to cover the land; it shall be in the latter days, and I will bring thee against My land, that the heathen may know Me, when I shall be sanctified in thee, O Gog, before their eyes. Thus saith the Lord GOD; Art thou he of whom I have spoken in old time by My servants the prophets of Israel, which prophesied in those days many years that I would bring thee against them? And it shall come to pass at the same time when Gog shall come against the land of Israel, saith the Lord GOD, that My fury shall come up in My face."

Ezekiel 38:1-18 unveils a major strike on the nation of Israel. These undertakings will occur at a set time in history as prophesied by the servants of the LORD. Turkey supplies Syria with logistic and political support while Russia owns and operates a naval base located in Tartus, Syria, which is approximately four hundred and thirty eight kilometers or two hundred and seventy-two miles from Israel. This is a very short distance to fire nuclear missile warheads into unsuspecting Israel and the size of the payload of these missiles will cause mass causalities. These coalition forces will come up against unsuspecting Israel by air, land and sea, utilizing a very well planned invasion. Ezekiel 38:9 states that the aftermath of these simultaneous strikes will overwhelm the Israeli military and air defense, and as a result, there will be great casualties; the aftermath leaving the air thick with smoke from the destruction.

South Arabia [Sheba]; Al-'Ula a city of Arabia [Dedan] and the merchants of Spain [Tarshish] will join with the other countries in the Middle East [young lions] to overrun Israel. Therefore, the whisking away of silver and gold, cattle, goods and great spoils; is symbolically referring to Israel's great and diversified enterprises. Ezekiel prophesied that at an appointed time in history when these things do occur, the military might of

Russia; the grandmaster of this war along with his Middle East confederates will be in for a rude awakening because it will be the Lord Himself who will lure them into the land of Israel like live bait. The presence of South Arabia in this conflict leaves one to surmise that the invasion of Israel is about oil and natural gas. This military coalition however, will be broken as the LORD God defends defeated Israel Himself. Realizing that there is a greater power that fights for the tiny democracy of Israel, all their enemies will be dumbfounded and everyone worldwide will be astonished. The Russian military, along with the might of Turkey and their allies, will not have time to retreat as the LORD arises in great fury and jealousy for His people.

Verses 19-23

"For in My jealousy and in the fire of My wrath have I spoken, Surely in that day there shall be a great shaking in the land of Israel; so that the fishes of the sea, and the fowls of the heaven, and the beasts of the field, and all creeping things that creep upon the earth, and all the men that are upon the face of the earth, shall shake at My presence, and the mountains shall be thrown down, and the steep places shall fall, and every wall shall fall to the ground. And I will call for a sword against him throughout all My mountains, saith the Lord GOD: every man's sword shall be against his brother. And I will plead against him with pestilence and with blood; and I will rain upon him, and upon his bands, and upon the many people that are with him, an overflowing rain, and great hailstones, fire, and brimstone. Thus will I magnify Myself, and sanctify Myself, and I will be known in the eyes of many nations, and they shall know that I am the LORD."

The LORD continues to unfold to Ezekiel His plans to defeat all nations that come against Israel and these signs will usher in the beginning of the end. Jerusalem will be taken during this battle of brethren against brethren, but a remnant of God's people will be saved from the mayhem by heading to a pre-determined place of safety. As war consumes the land of Israel; the LORD God will step in and defend His inheritance with a mighty earthquake [great shaking], so tremendous, that it will not be able to be measured on the Richter' scale. This earthquake will cause a polar shift. The earth's magnetic fields will be affected and the earth will wobble on its axis.

This wobbling of the earth will in turn, affect all creation both in the air, in the sea and on land. Mountains will plunge into the Mediterranean and massive lightning strikes will cause fires which will be fueled by the eruption of gas and oil mines. Tornadoes will be accompanied by giant size hailstones; tsunamis (overflowing rain) will cause massive flooding. There lies the possibility of volcanic eruptions with sulfuric stones (brimstones) raining down on the earth on this military leader and his allies as the two inactive volcanoes in the Golan Heights suddenly explodes accompanied by a cosmic bombardment similar to that which destroyed both cities of Sodom and Gomorrah (Genesis 19:24). The death toll from these catastrophic events will be astronomical and the enemies of Israel, who survives this cataclysmic event, will not escape the grip of death.

The stench of death will fill the air. Poor sanitation and contaminated water will force survivors to drink from pools infested with vermin that will transmit deadly diseases causing widespread epidemics. At this point all will know that these devastations were not by mere coincidence, because there is a God in Israel who informed Ezekiel of these things approximately seven hundred and fifty years before Yeshua Jesus came into this world. Who in their right mind will mark these events as an act of nature? The earth truly will shake; but it will not be by mother earth, but by FATHER GOD! This is only the beginning of their pain and suffering, the LORD has not finished punishing Israel's enemies. Russia will be in the news once again; just as they had many of Israel's cities razed by fire, so will the largest of their metropolitan cities be engulfed in flames as payment for the part they played in the plot against Israel.

Chapter 39

Verses 1-6

"Therefore, thou son of man, prophesy against Gog, and say, Thus saith the Lord GOD; Behold, I am against thee, O Gog, the chief prince of Meshech and Tubal: and I will turn thee back, and leave but the sixth part of thee, and will cause thee to come up from the north parts, and will bring thee upon the mountains of Israel: and I will smite thy bow out of thy left hand, and will cause thine arrows to fall out of thy right hand. Thou shalt fall upon the mountains of Israel, thou and thy bands, and the people that is with thee: I will give thee unto the ravenous birds of every sort, and to the beasts of the field to be devoured. Thou shalt fall upon the open field: for I have spoken it, saith the Lord GOD. And I will send a fire on Magog, and among them that dwell carelessly in the isles: and they shall know that I am the LORD."

The LORD directly speaks of a man who is most likely the political and military leader of Russia since he possesses the greatest influence over the other nations which lies north of Israel. In chapter 38:4 this nation would retreat being caught in a trap. What could this trap be? And why would this snare lure such a leader and military strategist? What did Israel possess that would have caused this renowned expert whom many seek for clever advise to drop his guard? It must be something that is considered a trophy; one not intended for the mantle of a fireplace or displayed in a well-fortified museum. This trophy will catapult Russia and Turkey into world dominance, exalted once more above all nations as he who possesses the most oil and natural gas boasts a strong economy and takes center stage among global leaders.

In 2009 the Tamar field in the Mediterranean Sea was discovered by the Israelis to contain natural gas deposits, which is the largest find since the Noble Energy Company began offshore drilling. By 2013, this company was producing an exceptionally large quantity of natural gas to the tune of three million cubic feet daily. It is also estimated that there is another ten trillion cubic feet of this natural fossil fuel yet to be tapped that has the potential of changing the geo-political and economic status of Israel, skyrocketing them to a place of prominence in the Middle East. The Leviathan basin is another prize in the hands of the Israelis. Located approximately eighty miles off the shores of Haifa, the Leviathan basin has the yielding capacity of another mind boggling sixteen trillion cubic feet of organic gas. Is this the hook that will lure Russian and Turkish leaders to take Israel at all cost? The game of chess is on, as the nation that holds the greatest oil and natural gas reserves will undoubtedly rule the world. Wars and rumors of war against Israel are directly related to oil; the thrust unmistakably is to own Israel, therefore all of its natural resources, but the LORD will overturn the plans of the crafty. Consider these sayings of the LORD recorded in Job 5:12-16 applying the NIV: "*He thwarts the plans of the crafty, so that their hands achieve no success. He catches the wise in their craftiness, and the schemes of the wily are swept away. Darkness comes upon them in the daytime; at noon they grope as in the night. He saves the needy from the sword in their mouth; he saves them from the clutches of the powerful. So the poor have hope and injustice shuts its mouth.*" The enemies of Israel will be driven back by the demonstration of the power of Almighty God and this He will do in Israel's behalf and when the smoke settles, only one sixth of Israel's enemy will remain.

There is so much said in Scripture about the organic gas deposit of the Leviathan basin, that leaves no doubt that the eyes of the superpowers are bent on possessing it for themselves. In Job chapter 41:1-34 the LORD God put forth a series of paradoxical questions to His servant that allude to this untapped source of organic gas called "*the beast,*" to demonstrate the veracity and extraordinary productivity of the Leviathan basin. Applying the paraphrased NLT the truth about this source of organic gas will be unsealed in layman's terms: "*Can you catch Leviathan with a hook or put a noose around its jaw? Can you tie with a rope through the nose or pierce its jaw with a spike? Will it beg you for mercy or implore you for pity? Will it agree to work for you, to be your slave for life? Can you make it a pet like a bird, or give it to your little girls to play with? Will merchants try to buy it to sell it in their shops? Will its hide be hurt by spears or its head by harpoon? If you lay a hand on it, you will certainly remember the battle that follows. You won't try that again! No, it is useless to try to capture it. The hunter who attempts it will be knocked down. And since no one dares to disturb it, who then can stand up to me? Who has given me anything that I need to pay back? Everything under heaven is mine. I want to emphasize Leviathan's limbs and its enormous strength and graceful form. Who can strip off its hide, and who can penetrate its double layer of armor? Who can pry open its jaws? For its teeth are terrible! The scales on its back are like rows of shields tightly sealed together. They are so close together that no air can get between them. Each scale sticks tight to the next. They interlock and cannot be penetrated. When it sneezes, it flashes light! Its eyes are like the red of dawn. Lightning leaps from its mouth; flames of fire flashes out smoke streams from its nostrils like steam from a pot heated over burning rushes. Its breath would kindle coals, for flames shoot from its mouth. The tremendous strength in Leviathan's neck strikes terror wherever it goes. Its flesh is hard and firm and cannot be penetrated. Its heart is hard as rock, hard as millstone. When it rises, the mighty are afraid, gripped by terror. No sword can stop it, no spear dart, or javelin. Iron is nothing but straw to that creature, and bronze is like rotten wood. Arrows cannot make it flee. Stones shot from a sling are like bits of grass. Clubs are like of grass, and it laughs at the swish of javelins. Its belly is covered with scales as sharp as glass. It plows up the ground as it drags through the mud. Leviathan makes the water boil with its commotion. It stirs the depths like a pot of ointment. The water glistens in its wake, making the sea look white. Nothing on earth is its equal, no other creature so fearless. Of all the creatures, it is the proudest. It is the king of beasts."* The Leviathan basin is like no other organic gas deposit on the planet and its vast supply is a mighty hook; a trophy among trophies that will draw the superpower leeches to possess it! Who then can control it, hasn't the LORD said it belongs to Him?

This determined group will attack Israel under false allegations to take this prized possession no matter the cost. At first they will not succeed because the Israelis will outsmart them. They will retreat and formulate a second plan using all the fighting power and coalition forces they have at their disposal. This time however, the LORD GOD of Israel who carved out the Leviathan basin will be ready with His own sophisticated weaponry. Israel will be attacked from its natural fortress of the mountains, but the LORD God will avenge them. The might of the aggressors will be routed for a second time and their bodies will be food for carnivorous birds and wild animals. Those who flee to the open field as well as those observing the war anticipating Israel's defeat, will be consumed by fire. The LORD God who destroyed Sodom and Gomorrah with sulfuric stones when there were no volcanoes nearby, will call upon His reserves in the heavens to do His bidding.

Verses 7-10

"So I will make My holy name known in the midst of My people Israel; and I will not let them pollute My holy name any more: and the heathen shall know that I am the LORD, the Holy One in Israel. Behold, it is come, and it is done, saith the Lord GOD; this is the day whereof I have spoken. And they that dwell in the cities of Israel shall go forth, and shall set on fire and burn the weapons, both the shields and the bucklers, the bows and the arrows, and the hand staves, and the spears, and they shall burn them with fire seven years: so that they shall take no wood out of the field, neither cut down any out of the forests; for they shall burn the weapons with fire: and they shall spoil those that spoiled them, and rob those that robbed them, saith the Lord GOD."

Not only will the enemies of Israel witness the demonstration of God's power over nature being unleashed, but the whole earth will view these happenings by satellite. The doubters, prognosticators, all heathens and even the Israel of God His chosen and elect will declare that there is but One true and living GOD. A specific date is written and proposed by the LORD for these things to occur. When they are fulfilled, those who once rejected the Holy Scriptures will frantically search through its pages and realize for themselves that truly there is no other book on the face of the earth that documents such marvelous prophesies. Many presumably sacred prophetic documents have been repeatedly redacted over the centuries but only the Word of God written by the inspiration of Holy Spirit through his trusted bondservants has withstood the test of time. Those who have foolishly rejected the Word of God will stand before a Righteous Judge and have the Word of God testify against them. The LORD God will defend His Holiness and His Holy Word.

This is the prophetic utterance of Zachariah a servant of the LORD whose ministry began more than five hundred years before Yeshua was born: "*A day of the LORD is about to come when your possessions will be divided as plunder in your midst. For I will gather all the nations against Jerusalem to wage war; the city will be taken, its houses plundered, and the women raped. Then half of the city will go into exile, but the remainder of the people will not be taken away. Then the LORD will go to battle and fight against those nations, just as he fought battles in ancient days. On that day his feet will stand on the Mount of Olives which lies to the east of Jerusalem, and the Mount of Olives will be split in half from east to west, leaving a great valley. Half the mountain will move northward and the other half southward. Then you will escape through the mountain valley, for the mountains will extend to Azal. Indeed, you will flee as you fled from the earthquake in the days of King Uzziah of Judah. Then the LORD my God will come with all his holy ones with him. On that day there will be no light the source of light in the heavens will congeal. It will happen in one day (a day known to the LORD); not in the day or in the night, but in the evening there will be light. Moreover, on that day living waters will flow out of Jerusalem, half of them to the eastern sea and half of them to the western sea; it will happen both in summer and in winter. The LORD will then be king over all the earth. In that day the LORD will be seen as one with a single name. All the land will change and become like the Arabah from Geba to Rimmon, south of Jerusalem; and Jerusalem will be raised up and will stay in its own place from Benjamin Gate to the site of the First Gate and on the Corner Gate, and from the Tower of Hananel to the royal winepress. And people will settle there, and there will no longer be the threat of divine extermination Jerusalem will dwell in security. But this will be the nature of the plague with which the LORD will strike all the nations that have fought against Jerusalem: Their flesh will decay while they stand on their feet, their eyes will rot away in their sockets, and their tongues will dissolve in their mouths. On that day there will be great confusion from the LORD among them; they will seize each other and attack one another violently. Moreover, Judah will fight at Jerusalem, and the wealth of all the surrounding nations will be gathered up gold, silver, and clothing in great abundance"* (14:1-14 NET (for further studies see Isaiah 40:1-5; Luke 3:5; Revelation 16:17-20)). It is not a matter of "if" these things will happen, but "when" these things will happen.

Calamity drives people to introspection, confession and repentance; and a gracious and forgiving Father offers all redemption. Those who have polluted the name of the Most High and oppressed His people will do so no more, because the LORD of Heavens Army will defeat their foes and the aftermath of this calamity will be a cleanup campaign for His people as one of King David's plea is answered. Psalm 14 applying the NET states: *"Fools say to themselves, 'There is no God.' They sin and commit evil deeds; none of them does what is right. The LORD looks down from heaven at the human race, to see if there is anyone who is wise and seeks God. Everyone rejects God; they are all morally corrupt. None of them does what is right, not even one! All those who behave wickedly do not understand, those who devour my people as if they were eating bread, and do not call out to the LORD. They are absolutely terrified, for God defends the godly. You want to humiliate the oppressed, even though the LORD is their shelter. I wish the deliverance of Israel would come from Zion! When the LORD restores the wellbeing of his people, may Jacob rejoice, may Israel be happy!"*

Throughout Israel's history, the LORD has raised up His ministers the prophets to warn His enemies but to no avail. Alarmingly, it usually takes catastrophic events to get the wicked to cry out to God in repentance. In Ezekiel 39:7-10 the LORD addresses His people first and promise to reveal His holy name to them, which will be the revelation of His character and an unveiling of His presence from the Most Holy Place. The Temple of God will be made sanctified, because Yeshua the High Priest will sanctify it Himself. There will be a spiritual awakening as the veil will be removed from the minds of unbelieving Jews who will proclaim "Yeshua is Lord." The heathens who have been humbled by all that they have both witnessed and heard, will also proclaim with the house of Israel that Yeshua is Lord! The Apostle Paul wrote these inspiring words: *"And this is God's plan: Both Gentiles and Jews who believe the Good News share equally in the riches inherited by God's children. Both are part of the same body, and both enjoy the promise of blessings because they belong to Christ Jesus"* (Ephesians 3:6 NLT).

Looking closely at Ezekiel 39:8 we will notice that it is written in the present tense: *"Behold, it is come, and it is done, saith the Lord GOD; this is the day whereof I have spoken."* This verse must be viewed in context with the previous verse which states: *"So will I make My holy name known in the midst of My people Israel;"* they are both speaking of a coming event since most of Israel is currently secular. The LORD goes on to say *"I will make My holy name known in the midst of My people Israel,"* which also points to the future as well as the second portion of verse seven: *"... I will not let them pollute My holy name any more."* Lastly in Ezekiel 39:7, the LORD addresses the heathens: *"... and the heathen shall know that I am the LORD, the Holy One in Israel."* Notice that He will reveal Himself to the Jews first, followed by His revelation to non-Jews. Romans 1:16 and 2:9-10 speaks of the punishment and also the glory that will come to the Jews first, followed by the Gentiles. The Lord said to Abraham: *"And I will make you a great nation, and I will bless you, and make your name great; and so you shall be a blessing; and I will bless those who bless you, and the one who curses you I will curse. And in you all the families of the earth will be blessed."* Psalm 33:12 is another Old Covenant reminder of the extended favor of God for all people: *"Blessed is the nation whose God is the LORD; and the people whom He hath chosen for His own inheritance"* (Genesis 12:2-3 NASB). A final showdown will come to the Middle East conflict as far as Israel is concerned.

All of Israel will know without a shadow of doubt that God is for them and not against them. They will arise in strength and finish the job which God had started. The people of Israel will set ablaze the diverse weapons left by their adversaries until the land is sanctified. All that was stolen from Israel will be restored. Ezekiel 39:10 states: *"So that they shall take no wood out of the field, neither cut down any out of the forests; for they shall burn the weapons with fire: and they shall spoil those that spoil them, and rob those that robbed them, saith the Lord GOD."* Symbolically "wood," speaks of humanity; at the end of this great battle the surviving enemies of Israel will surrender voluntarily without bloodshed.

In Ezekiel 39:10, the Hebrew word transliterated *"Field"* is **Sadheh** [7704]. Remarkably this word refers to a flat piece of land or the country whose modern day name is Syria. It can also be defined as the area of the Tigris-Euphrates river system shared by Iraq, Kuwait and the northeastern section of Syria collectively known as Mesopotamia. From this information regarding the understanding of the transliteration of the word *"Field"* or its

Hebrew counterpart **Sadheh**; one specific country of importance stands out above the rest and that is Syria which borders Israel to the northeast. Ezekiel 39:10 must therefore be interpreted as an idiomatic expression conveying the understanding that Syria's northeastern border will be compromised leading to its capture and annexation to Israel without bloodshed. The reason for purporting this belief is based on the idiomatic content of Ezekiel 39:10: "... *they shall take no wood [human] out of the field [region]; neither cut down [kill] any out of the forest [honeycomb].* The Hebrew word **Yaar** [3293] used for "forest," can also refer to the honeycomb. Interestingly there is something about the care of beehives by the Syrians that will reveal a fact about some of the residents living in the north-eastern border between Israel and Syria.

Syrian terracotta beehives were the first of its kind to be developed in the world. An average of about one hundred colonies per home is housed in pockets created in the walls to protect them from the extreme heat which is normal for the region. Another fact to consider is Northeastern Syria forms portion of the river plain of Al-Jazira, where many Assyrian Christians call home due to religious persecution. Could this be the reason why its capture will be a peaceful one? Is the honeycomb referring to the Christian settlers? Or is it symbolic of a place of protection during this period of unrest?

The fate of Syria has however been foretold by the Holy Bible. The final portion of Ezekiel 39:10 states: "... *they shall spoil those that spoil them, and rob those that robbed them, saith the Lord GOD."* Going back to Ezekiel 38:14-16: *Therefore, son of man, prophesy and say unto Gog, Thus saith the Lord GOD; in that day when My people of Israel dwelleth safely, shalt thou not know it? And thou shalt come from thy place **out of the north parts,** thou and many people with thee, all of them riding upon horses, a great company, and a mighty army: and thou shalt come up against My people of Israel, as a cloud to cover the land; it shall be in the latter days, and I will bring thee against My land, that the heathen may know Me, when I shall be sanctified in thee, O Gog, before their eyes."* Syria borders Israel to the north and this is the area where Russia, Turkey, and their allies will make a preemptive strike on Israel. Syria, as well as Lebanon, will be strategic points from which Israel will be simultaneously bombarded with an arsenal of weaponry including nuclear, as well as biological (see Zachariah 14:1-14).

The Hebrew word for "*field*" **Sadheh,** which also refers to Mesopotamia is of current prophetic interest. Places to keep a close eye on in this region are southwestern Turkey and southwestern Iran, the Tigris and Euphrates River system within Iraq, Kuwait and the northern portion of Syria; specifically Al-Jazira. This will be an all-out united effort by countries in or allied to the Middle Eastern bloc, and this revelation is based on Scriptural interpretation. Be reminded that this combat will play out just like a game of chess and that Russia is also a player on the board; they are not the planners or organizers of the game. As said before, big games are sponsored by big names, and their influence and financial support is geared to influence the outcome. These are the behind the scene moguls whose operations are clandestine, but there is the all-seeing One who will reveal all their secrets and foil their plans. Russia took center stage because they were considered to be the best to lead the planning of this war game, and for this reason they will be severely punished by the LORD.

Verses 11-16

"And it shall come to pass in that day, that I will give unto Gog a place there of graves in Israel, the valley of the passengers on the east of the sea: and it shall stop the noses of the passengers: and there shall they bury Gog and all his multitude: and they shall call it the valley of Hamongog. And seven months shall the house of Israel be burying of them, that they may cleanse the land. Yea, all the people of the land shall bury them; and it shall be to them a renown the day that I shall be glorified, saith the Lord GOD. And they shall sever out men of continual employment, passing through the land to bury with the passengers those that remain upon the face of the earth, to cleanse it: after the end of seven months shall they search. And the passengers that pass through the land, when any seeth a man's bone, then shall he set up a sign by it, till the buriers have buried it in the valley of Hamongog. And also the name of the city shall be Hamonah. Thus shall they cleanse the land."

Ezekiel was told of the great unrest that would consume the Middle East hundreds of years in advance. Ecclesiastes 3:11

and Isaiah 46:9-10 applying the NET states: "*God has made everything fit beautifully in its appropriate time, but he has also placed ignorance in the human heart so that people cannot discover what God has ordained, from the beginning to the end of their life. . . . Remember what I have accomplished in antiquity! Truly I am God, I have no peer; I am God, and there is none like me, who announces the end from the beginning and reveals beforehand what has not yet occurred, who says, "My plan will be realized, I will accomplish what I desire."* The creator of time knows its expiration date, because all that will transpire in the heavens and upon the earth is inscribed in His being.

Ezekiel's prophecies are being revealed because these are the times for their unveiling. In the final hour of human history this possessed prince and power of darkness will appear to be winning as he checkmates Israel because he studies the ways of men and knows their strengths and most importantly their weaknesses. The prince although very clever at what he does, will be no match for the greatest chess player of all time; Abba Father his creator! The LORD will intervene when it seems as if evil has the upper hand, and save the day. Israel will be redeemed and the body of Yeshua Jesus will find rest in Him that is faithful.

The grave of this prince will be in the dust of Israel and the exact location of his fall revealed: the Valley of the Passengers. Here is somewhat of a mystery; the Valley of the Passengers is located in modern day Jordan, which means this portion of land will also be captured by Israel (see verse 10). These demon possessed military leaders from the land of Russia, Turkey and their allied forces, will be buried in the Valley of the Passengers. Psalm 83:13-18 states: "*O my God, scatter them like tumbleweed, like chaff before the wind! As a fire burns a forest and as a flame sets mountains ablaze, chase them with your fierce storm; terrify them with your tempest. Utterly disgrace them until they submit to your name, O LORD. Let them be ashamed and terrified forever. Let them die in disgrace. Then they will learn that you alone are called LORD, that you alone are the Most High, supreme over all the earth*" (NLT). Israel is seen here advancing and defeating their enemies, reclaiming old forgotten lands which were once a part of Israel and promised to Abraham by GOD Himself.

Strewn over the Valley of the Passengers will be putrefied human remains. The overwhelming stench of decaying bodies blown by the hot wind will pollute the air. Passersby will cover their nose because of the unbearable yet distinct odor of the putrefied corpse of men. Many will be employed to thoroughly cleanse the valley for seven months and sanctify it unto the LORD. We must understand that the perfect number is seven and signifies the purification of the land not unto men but unto God, and the cleansing of the land is its rededication unto Him. The prophet Isaiah said: *"Thus says the LORD, the Holy One of Israel, and his Maker: "Ask Me of things to come concerning My sons; and concerning the work of My hands, you command Me. I have made the earth, and created man on it. I - My hands - stretched out the heavens, and all their host I have commanded. I have raised him up in righteousness, and I will direct all his ways; he shall build My city and let My exiles go free, not for price nor reward." Says the LORD of hosts. Thus says the LORD: "The labor of Egypt and merchandise of Cush and of the Sabeans, men of stature, shall come over to you, and they shall be yours; they shall walk behind you, they shall come over in chains; and they shall bow down to you. They will make supplication to you, saying, "Surely God is in you, and there is no other; there is no other God,' " Truly you are God, who hide Yourself, O God of Israel, the Savior! They shall be ashamed and also disgraced, all of them; they shall go in confusion together, who are makers of idols. But Israel shall be saved by the LORD with an everlasting salvation; you shall not be ashamed or disgraced forever and ever. For thus says the LORD, who created the heavens, who is God, who formed the earth and made it, who has established it, who did not create it in vain, who formed it to be inhabited: "I am the LORD, and there is no other. I have not spoken in secret, in a dark place of the earth; I did not say to the seed of Jacob, 'Seek Me in vain'; I, the LORD, speak in righteousness, I declare things that are right"* (45:11-19 NKJV).

Under Israel's new government the Valley of the Passengers will be renamed Hamongog; interpreted multitude or horde of Gog. This term refers to all the enemies of Israel, for they are of one mind, one mandate and one mission. This piece of real estate will be a memorial of the mighty acts of the LORD God on behalf of His people. The name of the city will be changed to Hamonah which is interpreted "multitude" as sworn by the LORD. Hamonah is modern day Dhiban located in west-central Jordan. The small town of Hamonah is approximately forty-three miles or seventy kilometers south of Amman Jordan and just east of the Dead Sea in the Madaba Governorate; it has a current population of over fifteen thousand, the majority of whom are employed by the military!

In 1868 the Mesha Stele inscription also known as the Moabite stone, was found by a German missionary named F. A. Klein in Dhiban. Mesha was a Moabite King who recorded his own rebellion against the King of Israel after defaulting on payment of tribute money. The information of this king's defiance against Israel is recorded in 2 Kings 3:1-5 quoting from the NASB that states: "*Now Jehoram the son of Ahab became king over Israel at Samaria in the eighteenth year of Jehoshaphat king of Judah, and reigned twelve years. He did evil in the sight of the LORD, though not like his father and his mother, for he put away the sacred pillar of Baal which his father had made. Nevertheless he clung to the sins of Jeroboam the son of Nebat, which he made Israel sin; he did not depart from them. Now Mesha king of Moab was a sheep breeder and used to pay the king of Israel 100,000 lambs and the wool of 100,000 rams. But when Ahab died, the king of Moab rebelled against the king of Israel.*" Israel now occupies only a small fraction of the land that was given to them by the LORD (see also Joshua chapters 12-17; Judge 3:1-4). The twelve tribes failed to thoroughly cleanse the land and so fell into idolatrous practices. They married the daughters of the heathens and lost most of their inheritance because of their sins and transgressions against Abba Father. These lands will one day be restored to Israel as the Lord GOD had purposed in His heart to give them as stated by Ezekiel 39:10. The original boundaries of Israel will be reinstated as the house of Israel unites as one under Yeshua Messiah.

Verses 17-20

"*And, thou son of man, thus saith the Lord GOD; Speak unto every feathered fowl, and to every beast of the field, assemble yourselves, and come; gather yourselves on every side to My sacrifice that I do sacrifice for you, even a great sacrifice upon the mountains of Israel, that ye may eat flesh, and drink blood. Ye shall eat the flesh of the mighty, and drink the blood of the princes of the earth. Of rams, of lambs, and of goats, of bullocks, all of them fatlings of Bashan. And ye shall eat fat till ye be full, and drink blood till ye be drunken, of My sacrifice which I have sacrificed for you. Thus ye shall be filled at My table with horses and chariots, with mighty men of war, saith the Lord GOD."*

As we have seen repeatedly in the book of Ezekiel the LORD sometimes speaks to the prophet by painting a picture with words. In so doing the force and intent of His discourse adds depth to His point of view. In Ezekiel 39:17, this same method of communicating a point is used. *"Speak unto every feathered fowl,"* or *"to every beast of the field;"* both terms are euphemisms. "Every feathered fowl" is interpreted as diverse nations, while "every beast," is the Hebrew word **Chay** [2416], which infers unity of purpose: body, soul and spirit with one objective. As previously stated the word translated for *"field"* **Sadheh** [7704], refers to either a plain, Syria, or the conglomerates of Mesopotamia that shares the area of the Tigris-Euphrates river system; which is Syria, Iraq, and Kuwait. Notice however, that Syria was mentioned separately and again included with the group. The analysis of Ezekiel 39:7-10 highlighted Syria. Iraq has already been humbled and Kuwait, which means "fortress," an ally of Syria is also on the radar of the LORD. The term "every beast of the field," would indicate that all three countries will be sanctioned by the LORD. This is not a personal opinion but a revelation unveiled by the transliteration of these Hebrew words, which reveals a panorama of the prophetic interpretation of the Word of God. Nations, who hold steadfast to the opinion that the Bible is corrupt, cannot argue with the Hebraic Text from which these revelations have been unearthed.

All is not gloom and doom for the Middle East, one day a great spiritual awakening will envelope its people. The LORD offers the descendants of both Ishmael and Esau a personal invitation to attend His sacrifice. A portion of Ezekiel 39:17 is underlined below with its assigned Hebraic number that will be used to reveal a deeper meaning of the verse: *"Gather yourselves on every side to My sacrifice [2077] that I do sacrifice [2076] for you, even a great sacrifice [2077] upon the mountains of Israel, that ye may eat flesh [1320] and drink blood [1818]".* Here we see the assembly of nations summoned by the LORD God of Israel. He gathers them specifically for a burnt offering; "My sacrifice," **Zevach** [2077]. Old Covenant burnt offerings were classified as one of the most important offerings unto the LORD. These offerings were voluntary, made by fire upon the brazen (bronze) altar morning and evening (see Leviticus 1:1-

17; 8:18-21; 16:24). The main purpose of this offering was an act of worship, because the entire sacrifice was to be burnt upon the altar, therefore, no portion of it is eaten by the priest. The burnt offering signifies ones' expression of devotion and complete surrender to Almighty God and his earnest request for the forgiveness of unintentional sin. This is the meaning in a nutshell of "My sacrifice;" *Zevach*.

The next use of the word, "I do sacrifice," *Zavach* [2076]; (spelled with an "**a**") is extremely important. *Zavach* refers to the actual killing of the animal for sacrifice which is brought by the one who offers it. In this instance, it is the Lord GOD who brings the animal to be sacrificed. "Lord GOD" is here in its plural form, therefore speaking of the offering of Yeshua Messiah by His Father! Isaiah 53:6, 7 and 1 Peter 1:18-21 states: "*All we like sheep have gone astray; we have turned every one to his own way; and the LORD hath laid on Him the iniquity of us all. He was oppressed, and He was afflicted, yet He opened not His mouth: He is brought as a lamb to the slaughter, and as a sheep before her shearers is dumb, so He openeth not His mouth. . . . Forasmuch as ye know that ye were not redeemed with corruptible things, as silver and gold, from your vain conversation received by tradition from your fathers; but with the precious blood of Christ, as of a lamb without blemish and without spot: who verily was foreordained before the foundation of the world, but was manifest in these last times for you.*" This is Abba Father's personal offering which Yeshua voluntarily gives back to His Father as an act of His complete surrender, devotion and worship, being the perfect sacrifice and atonement for the sins of mankind. He laid down His life voluntarily thereby reconciling us to His Father. Yeshua Jesus said: "*For God so loved the world that He gave His only begotten Son, that whosoever believes in Him should not perish but have everlasting life. . . I am the good shepherd; and I know My sheep, and am known by My own. As the Father knows Me, even so I know the Father; and I lay down My life for the sheep. And other sheep I have which are not of this fold; them also I must bring, and they will hear My voice; and there will be one flock and one shepherd. Therefore My Father loves Me, because I lay down My life that I may take it again. No one takes it from Me, but I lay it down Myself, I have power to lay it down, and I have power to take it again. This command I have received from My Father*" (John 3:16; 10:14-18 NKJV).

Yeshua Jesus obediently offers Himself; He became our sacrifice, **Zavach** who was presented by Abba Father for the redemption of both Jews and Gentiles. The Lord GOD explicitly states in Ezekiel 39:17 that this was His sacrificial offering for the nations. Burnt offerings were for unintentional sin; therefore we see the unfolding of GOD'S abounding grace. Following the unveiling of the miraculous defense of Israel and the city of Jerusalem, many unbelievers will finally realize that Abba Father is the only GOD, and that Yeshua Jesus is truly His Son. Jerusalem's rightful owner will judge and His judgment is true!

Jerusalem is the religious capital of the world for Jews, Muslims and Christians alike. Located in a mountainous region of Israel, Jerusalem is separated from the Mount of Olives by the Valley of Jehoshaphat which means Abba Father shall judge. Joel 3:1-2 states: "*For behold, in those days, and in that time, when I shall bring again the captivity of Judah and Jerusalem. I will also gather all nations, and will bring them down into the valley of Jehoshaphat, and will plead with them there for My people and for My heritage Israel, whom they have scattered among the nations, and parted My land.*" The appointed times for the fulfillment of these prophesies are very close at hand and the city of Jerusalem, the Mount of Olives along with the valley of Jehoshaphat will be the center of it all. However, the eyes of the world will be upon the city of Jerusalem itself; the nucleus of religious controversy known to man; it is from this city that the atoning sacrifices from the Overcomers will ascend to heaven. Because Yeshua Messiah has already paid the sin ransom, this sacrifice will be one of thanksgiving and praise offered from the lips by the Israel of God. It is recorded in Galatians 6:15 and applying the NLT: "*It doesn't matter whether we have been circumcised or not. What counts is whether we have been transformed into a new creation.*"

Lastly we will examine the expression, "*eat My flesh*" [H. 1320 **Basar**] and "*drink My blood*" [H. 1818 **Dam**]. "Flesh is in reference to kinship, so "eat My flesh" used in context is referring to the destruction or wasting of God's heritage who are the Jews. "Drink My blood" is not referring to the consumption of blood but the death toll due to warfare. The expression, "*eat My flesh* [**Basar**] *and drink My blood* [**Dam**],*"* is interpreted: The willful taking of the life of a brother through the act of violence. This would indicate that it was the carnage of Yeshua's brethren being referred to here. The enemies of Israel will kill the valiant men (the mighty), civilian leaders (princes of the earth), political leaders (rams), citizens (lambs), leaders of the people (goats), protesters (bullocks). This slaughter will be at the hands of those who exert arbitrary or tyrannical authority from their portion of the Golan Heights located in Syria (all of the fatlings from Bashan). It must be stressed that these interpretations are not by conjecture but by the examination of the Hebrew root translation and transliteration of the English version of the Bible, which reveals a fresh prophetic view.

The outpouring of the judgment of God in defense of Israel will cause much perplexity for them, as well as their enemies and their victory will parallel that of the battle between Gideon and the Medianites because this battle will be won by Israel the ones expected to lose (Judges 7). Zechariah 14:3 states: *"Then the LORD will go forth and fight against those nations as when He fights on a day of battle"* (NASB). With all the hatred for Israel by extremist factions, God is still gracious and will forgive their sins committed through ignorance. Even after the great bloodshed the Lord GOD offers mercy: **Zavach**, which is the finished work of Yeshua Jesus, Abba Father's perfect sacrifice.

At this offering Israel's enemies both great and small will be ashamed of their wanton acts of evil. On the other hand, unbelieving Jews will know that Yeshua their brethren is Lord and that Abba Father is not against them. Hebrews 2:9-18 applying the NKJV states: *"But we see Jesus, who was made a little lower than angels, for the suffering of death crowned with glory and honor, that He by the grace of God, might taste death for everyone. For it was fitting for Him, for whom are all things, in bringing many sons to glory, to make the captain of their salvation perfect through sufferings. For both He who sanctifies and those who are being sanctified are all of one, for which reason He is not ashamed to call them brethren, saying: "I will declare Your name to My brethren; in the midst of the assembly I will sing praise to You." And again: "I will put My trust in Him." And again: 'Here am I and the children whom God has given Me." Inasmuch then as the children have partaken of flesh and blood, He Himself likewise shared in the same, that through death He might destroy him who had the power of death, that is the devil, and release those who through fear of death were all their lifetime subject to bondage. For indeed He does not give aid to angels, but He does give aid to the seed of Abraham. Therefore in all things He had to be made like His brethren, that He might be a merciful and faithful High Priest in things pertaining to God, to make propitiation for the sins of the people. For in that He Himself has suffered, being tempted, He is able to aid those who are tempted* (see also Psalm 22:22; Romans 8:28-39). In Ezekiel chapter thirty-nine, the Lord GOD invites the remainder of Abraham's descendants to partake in the same propitiatory atonement of reconciliation through the sacrificial offering of Yeshua Jesus for all!

Verses 21-29

"And I will set My glory among the heathen, and all the heathen shall see My judgment that I have executed, and My hand that I have laid upon them. So the house of Israel shall know that I am the LORD their God from that day and forward. And the heathen shall know that the house of Israel went into captivity for their iniquity: because they trespassed against Me, therefore hid I My face from them, and gave them into the hand of their enemies: so fell they by the sword. According to their uncleanness and according to their transgressions have I done unto them, and hid My face from them. Therefore thus saith the Lord GOD; Now will I bring again the captivity of Jacob, and have mercy upon the whole house of Israel, and will be jealous for My holy name.; after that they have borne their shame, and all their trespasses whereby they have trespassed against Me, when they dwelt safely in their land, and none made them afraid. When I have brought them again from the people, and gathered them out of their enemies' lands, and am sanctified in them in the sight of many nations; then shall they know that I am the LORD their God, which caused them to be led into captivity among the heathen: but I have gathered them unto their own land, and have left none of them any more there. Neither will I hide My face any more from them: for I have poured out My Spirit upon the house of Israel, saith the Lord GOD."

The original land previously allotted to the twelve tribes was much larger than what is now considered the State of Israel. Yeshua is Israel's true owner and only hope. He is betrothed to them and those who have accepted Him will also be accepted by Abba Father. One day Yeshua will return and declare His Sovereignty. Israel will flourish as believing Jews declare Yeshua as Savior and Lord. The sons of Jacob have obtained the favor of GOD above all people by bringing them back as promised to the soil of their inheritance. There will be tears of joy when Israel truly understand that they are chosen, loved and redeemed by the Lord GOD who sanctifies them in Himself. Holy Spirit the Ruach HaKodesh, who has always been with Israel, will be poured out upon them once again when all twelve tribes are finally re-gathered as one people.

This re-gathering will occur on the day of Shavuot, which is also known as the Feast of Weeks or Pentecost. Israel will be re-established in peace by the Prince of Peace: Yeshua Messiah whom Gentile believers call Jesus! This day will catapult Israel into her future renewal. As the temple of the LORD is being rebuilt in Israel, so will the temple of God be reestablished in man. What a glorious temple that will be as we will see unfolding brick by brick in volume three of this work. Philippians 3:20-21 applying the NKJV sates: "*For our citizenship is in heaven, from which we also eagerly wait for the Savior, the Lord Jesus Christ, who will transform our lowly body that it may be conformed to His glorious body, according to the working by which He is able even to subdue all things to Himself.*" The revelations to be discovered in volume three of this work will forever transform the life of the seeker of truth as Abba Father takes the temple of man and through the unending work of Holy Spirit, transform it into a holy temple, His perfect tabernacle, and most important of all, a dwelling place for the final rest of the glory of the LORD.

www.ingramcontent.com/pod-product-compliance
Lightning Source LLC
Chambersburg PA
CBHW052011090426
42741CB00008B/1640